EYEWITNESS
AMAZON

Muisca figure made of gold

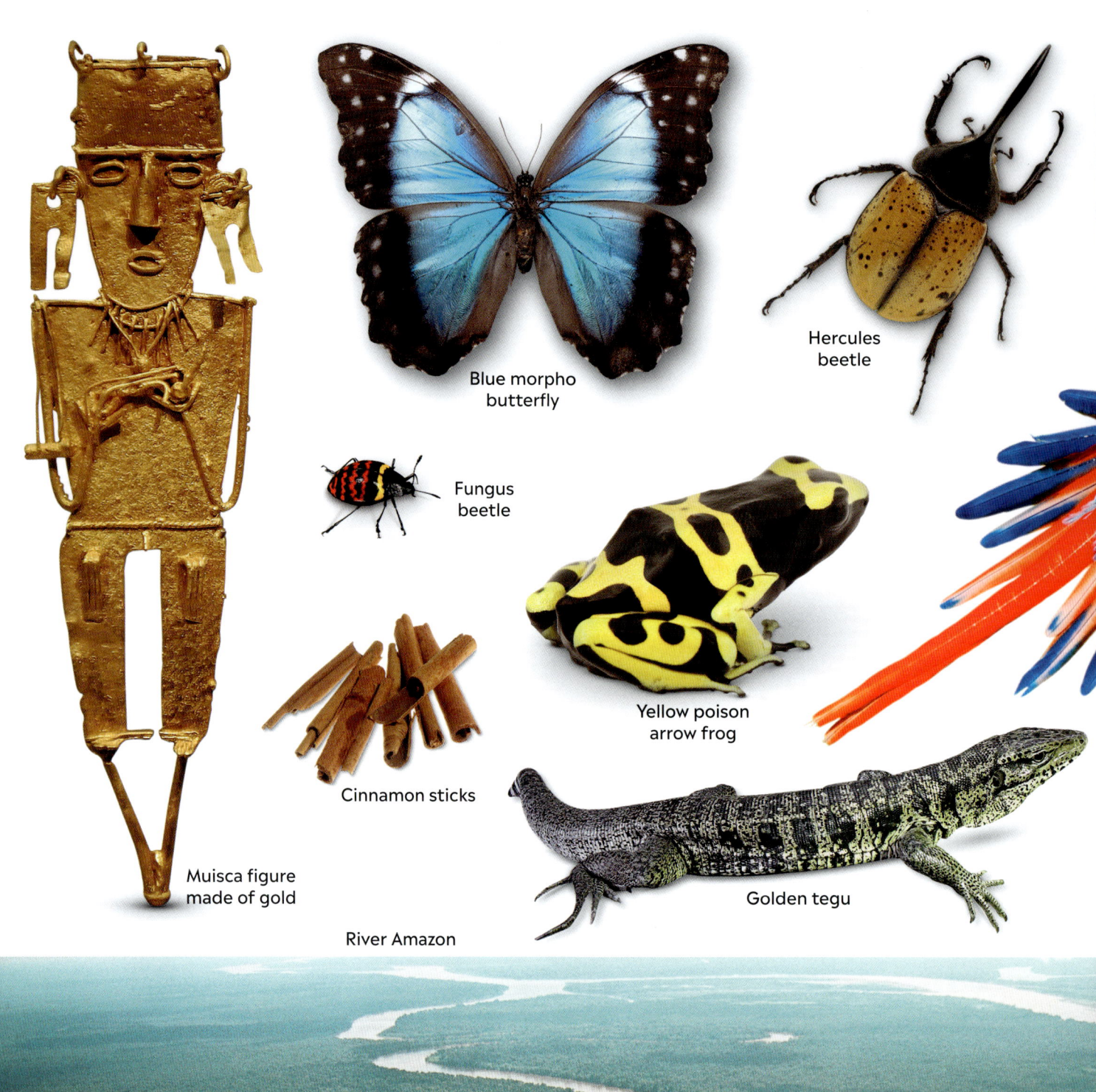

Blue morpho butterfly

Hercules beetle

Fungus beetle

Cinnamon sticks

Yellow poison arrow frog

Golden tegu

River Amazon

EYEWITNESS
AMAZON

Written by
TOM JACKSON

Macaw

Paradise tanager

Golden lion tamarin

DK

Green-billed toucan

Vine snake

REVISED EDITION

DK DELHI
Senior Editor Sreshtha Bhattacharya
Senior Art Editor Vikas Chauhan
Editor Bipasha Roy **Art Editors** Noopur Dalal, Aparajita Sen
Assistant Editor Mrinal Pant
Assistant Art Editor Anastasia Baliyan
DTP Designers Harish Aggarwal, Pawan Kumar, Vikram Singh
Picture Researcher Vishal Ghavri
Managing Editor Kingshuk Ghoshal
Managing Art Editor Govind Mittal
Jacket Designer Gayatri Menon
Senior Jackets Coordinator Priyanka Sharma Saddi

DK LONDON
Editor Kelsie Besaw **Art Editor** Chrissy Barnard
Managing Editor Francesca Baines
Managing Art Editor Philip Letsu
Production Editor Jacqueline Street-Elkayam
Senior Production Controller Jude Crozier
Jacket Design Development Manager Sophia MTT
Publisher Andrew Macintyre
Associate Publishing Director Liz Wheeler
Art Director Karen Self
Publishing Director Jonathan Metcalf

Consultant Michael Leach

FIRST EDITION

DK DELHI
Editorial team Bharti Bedi, Priyaneet Singh
Design team Pooja Pipil, Tanvi Sahu, Nidhi Rastogi, Nishesh Batnagar
DTP Designers Nityanand Kumar, Pawan Kumar
Picture Researcher Aditya Katyal
Jacket Designer Suhita Dharamjit
Managing Editor Kingshuk Ghoshal **Managing Art Editor** Govind Mittal

DK LONDON
Senior Editor Chris Hawkes **Senior Art Editor** Spencer Holbrook
Jacket Editor Claire Gell **Jacket Designer** Laura Brim
Jacket Design Development Manager Sophia MTT
Producer, Pre-production Luca Frassinetti **Producer** Gemma Sharpe
Managing Editor Linda Esposito **Managing Art Editor** Philip Letsu
Publisher Andrew Macintyre
Associate Publishing Director Liz Wheeler
Design Director Stuart Jackman
Publishing Director Jonathan Metcalf

Consultant John Woodward

This Eyewitness® Book has been conceived by
Dorling Kindersley Limited and Editions Gallimard

This edition published in 2022
First published in Great Britain in 2015 by
Dorling Kindersley Limited
DK, One Embassy Gardens, 8 Viaduct Gardens,
London, SW11 7BW

The authorised representative in the EEA is
Dorling Kindersley Verlag GmbH. Arnulfstr. 124,
80636 Munich, Germany

Copyright © 2015, 2022 Dorling Kindersley Limited
A Penguin Random House Company
10 9 8 7 6 5 4 3 2 1
001-331877-Dec/2022

All rights reserved.
No part of this publication may be reproduced, stored in
or introduced into a retrieval system, or transmitted,
in any form, or by any means (electronic, mechanical,
photocopying, recording, or otherwise), without the
prior written permission of the copyright owner.

A CIP catalogue record for this book
is available from the British Library.
ISBN: 978-0-2415-6984-9

Printed and bound in China

For the curious
www.dk.com

This book was made with Forest Stewardship
Council™ certified paper – one small step in
DK's commitment to a sustainable future.
For more information go to
www.dk.com/our-green-pledge

Pineapple   Passion fruit

Palm oil and fruits

Green and black poison dart frog

Amazonian children on a traditional canoe

Ocelot

Contents

Gold mask from Colombia

6 The Amazon
8 The Amazon Basin
10 The River Amazon
12 Land of forests
14 Around the rainforest
16 Wetlands
18 Plants and fungi
20 Birds of the Amazon
22 Amazon monkeys
24 On the forest floor
26 Creepy crawlies
28 In and around the river
30 Hunting for food
32 Of both worlds
34 Forest reptiles
36 Amazon fish
38 Ancient civilizations
40 Exploration and exploitation

42 Myths
44 Traditional life
46 Modern Amazonia
48 Getting around
50 Deforestation
52 Mining and damming
54 Endangered species
56 Modern industry
58 Conservation
60 Ecotourism
62 Farming
64 Amazon wonders
66 Amazon facts
68 Amazon by country
70 Glossary
72 Index

The Amazon

The Amazon is the site of the world's largest rainforest and its biggest river system. The Amazon Rainforest contains some large cities, and ancient settlements also exist deeper in the jungle. The amazing wildlife and geography, and a wealth of culture – ancient and modern – make the region one of Earth's greatest treasures.

Rainforest climate

The Amazon, like most rainforests around the world, is in a region called the tropics – the land that lies between the Tropics of Cancer and Capricorn. In the tropics, it is hot all year round, and it rains a lot. Parts of the Amazon Rainforest get 3.5 m (11.5 ft) of rain every year. All this heat and water makes it possible for dense jungles to grow.

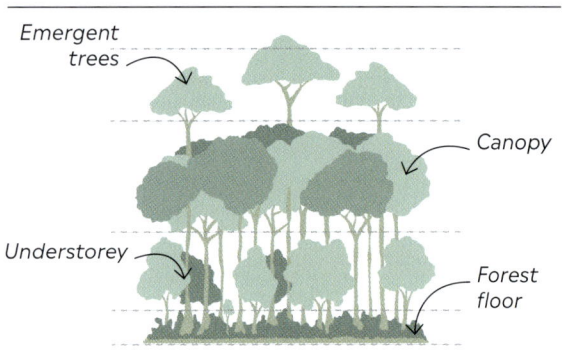

RAINFOREST LAYERS

- Emergent trees
- Canopy
- Understorey
- Forest floor

A rainforest has four layers: the dark, damp "forest floor", the "understorey" with a loose layer of smaller trees, the higher "canopy" layer where most fruits, flowers, and animals can be found, and the topmost "emergent" layer, where macaws and eagles may be spotted.

- Toco toucan
- Black caiman
- Blue morpho butterfly
- Agouti

Modern cities

The Amazon Rainforest contains several big cities. Iquitos, in Peru, is one of the largest. It is home to 484,000 people, and is just like any modern city – with parks, cinemas, and a sports stadium. The main difference is that the city is surrounded by the rainforest, and there are no highways linking it to the next town.

It's a jungle out there

The Amazon Rainforest is one of the most diverse habitats on Earth. One in 10 of the world's animal and plant species lives in its forests and rivers. Some animals, such as monkeys, seldom leave the tangle of branches, while plenty more live beside the shallow rivers. Others spend their entire lives on the forest floor.

Labels: Scarlet macaw, Emergent tree, Blue and yellow macaw, Howler monkey, Three-toed sloth, Emerald tree boa, Giant otter, Capybara, Giant waterlily, Jaguar, Green iguana

The Amazon Basin

The Amazon Rainforest exists because of South America's unique climate and geography. Storms from the Atlantic Ocean travel inland to produce rain on a vast, bowl-shaped area known as the Amazon Basin. Like a basin in a bathroom, it collects all the rain. Some of the water soaks into the forest floor, some of it evaporates and keeps the air damp, and the rest gushes into rivers that join to form the Amazon River.

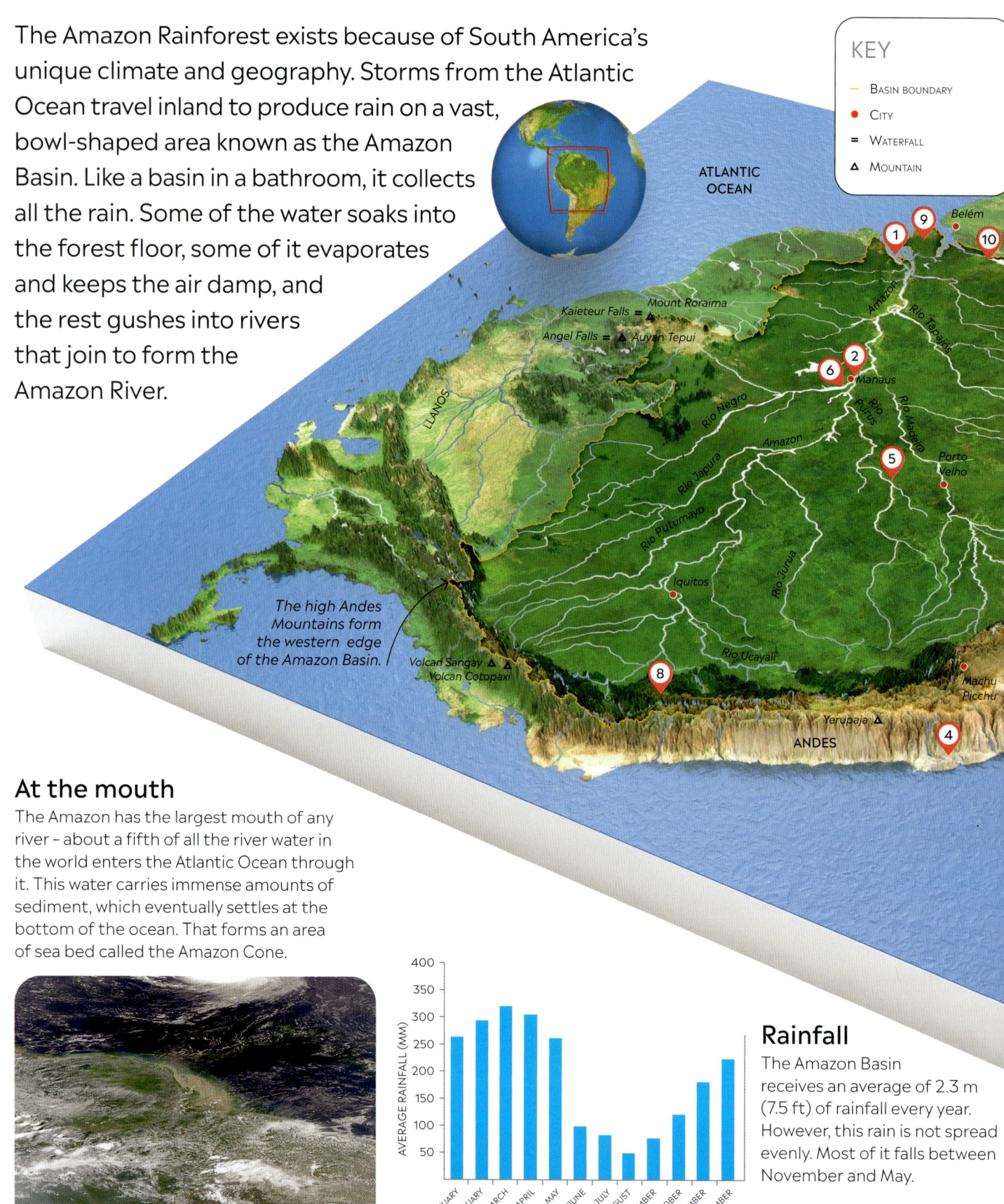

KEY
— Basin boundary
● City
= Waterfall
△ Mountain

At the mouth

The Amazon has the largest mouth of any river – about a fifth of all the river water in the world enters the Atlantic Ocean through it. This water carries immense amounts of sediment, which eventually settles at the bottom of the ocean. That forms an area of sea bed called the Amazon Cone.

Rainfall

The Amazon Basin receives an average of 2.3 m (7.5 ft) of rainfall every year. However, this rain is not spread evenly. Most of it falls between November and May.

Expansive region
The Amazon Basin covers 40 per cent of South America. The basin is surrounded by hills, mountains, and grassland. Every drop of rain that falls inside this area enters the Amazon River system.

Kaieteur Falls
Most of the Amazon Basin is very flat, so waterfalls and rapids are rare. The biggest waterfall inside the Basin is the Kaieteur Falls in the Guiana Highlands. Here, the water drops from a height of 226 m (741 ft), more than four times the height of the Niagara Falls.

Basin soil
The soil in the Amazon Basin is thin and does not contain many nutrients. Most fertile soils are filled with organic material that forms from the remains of dead plants and animals. This is not the case in the Amazon region. Here, fungi and bacteria recycle these substances so quickly that they are absorbed immediately by the roots of living plants.

The soil has a reddish tinge because of its iron content.

POINTS OF INTEREST

1. **Tidal bore** — A wave up to 4 m (13 ft) high that rushes upriver at high tide.
2. **Meeting of the waters** — The Rio Negro's dark waters meet the muddy Amazon River here.
3. **Nevado Mismi** — The source of the Amazon River in the Peruvian Andes.
4. **Nazca Lines** — Ancient patterns cut into the desert by the Nazca people.
5. **Lábrea** — One end of the Trans-Amazonian Highway (runs through the forest).
6. **Rio Negro Bridge** — The first major road bridge to cross a river in the region.
7. **Carajás Mine** — The largest iron ore mine in the world.
8. **Kuelap** — An ancient fortress built by the Chachapoya people.
9. **Marajó Island** — The largest river island in the world.
10. **Tucuruí Dam** — A huge power plant built across the Rio Tocantins.

Drought in the basin
These fishermen from Marajó Island, on the Amazon River, have nowhere to paddle their boat. In July and August, the water level around the Amazon River's mouth drops because of less rain further upstream.

The River Amazon

The Amazon River is the largest river in the world. It is around 6,516 km (4,049 miles) long, from its source in the Andes to its mouth in the Atlantic. The water flows from west to east, and eventually divides to form a huge 325-km- (202-mile-) wide estuary near Macapá, Brazil. Here, the river empties enough water into the Atlantic Ocean to fill 5,000 Olympic swimming pools every minute.

Meeting of the waters
The Amazon River's largest tributary is the Rio Negro, or "black river". Its water is filled with chemicals washed out of soil and plants, which make it very dark. It joins the Amazon near the Brazilian city of Manaus, but the waters of the two rivers do not mix for a few kilometres, creating a two-tone river.

The river sea
The Amazon contains so much water – more than any other river in the world – that it is more like a sea than a river. The main channel is about 50 m (164 ft) deep, and can be more than 10 km (6.2 miles) wide when flooded by heavy rains.

Many branches

The Amazon River flows from Peru to the Atlantic coast of Brazil. Along the way, it is joined by about 1,100 tributaries, many of which are huge rivers. The Madeira, Negro, and Paraná Rivers, for example, each carry more water than any river in Europe or North America. At its mouth, the Amazon again splits up into several channels, creating the world's largest river islands; the biggest, Marajó, is roughly the size of Switzerland.

EYEWITNESS

Picuruta Salazar

Top surfers come to ride the Amazon River's tidal bore – a wave created by ocean tides in the river's wide mouth. Locals call this wave *pororoca*, meaning "great roar". In 2003, Brazilian surfer Picuruta Salazar rode it for 37 minutes, covering more than 12 km (7.5 miles), and created a world record. The wave hit heights of 4 m (13 ft).

A satellite image of the mouth of the Amazon River

River dolphin

The tucuxi, an Amazon river dolphin, follows the river out to the Atlantic Ocean. Some groups of tucuxi have even been found living near Rio de Janeiro, more than 2,500 km (1,553 miles) to the south.

Land of forests

The Amazon Basin contains the world's largest tropical forest – 10 times the size of Spain. Most of the basin is covered in lowland rainforest, which gets plenty of rain, so the trees here grow faster and taller than anywhere else in South America. This region is also home to other types of forest, depending on climate and geography.

Palm
Along the southern edge of the Amazon Rainforest, where it is a little drier, the forest is dominated by palm trees. The most common type of palm is the babassu, which local people use both as a building material and as a source of food.

Dry forests
The arid highland areas around the edge of the Amazon Rainforest are covered in caatinga, meaning "white forest" in the local language – a reference to the area's dry, sandy soil. Only small trees and thorny shrubs can grow here. Other areas that are too dry for full forests are covered in cerrado, the Brazilian word for savannah.

Cloud forest
Mountain forests are also known as "cloud forests", as they are often shrouded in thick fog. The weather on mountain slopes is different from that in the lowlands: it rains less, and the temperature is lower. The trees there do not grow tall, and are often covered in mosses and creepers.

Woody vines

Lianas are thick, woody vines that grow up from the ground using the branches of trees to support them. Once it reaches sunlight, a liana spreads out, running from tree to tree, sprouting leafy branches. A liana forest grows in places in which trees are widely spaced, and the vines can fill the gaps between them.

Underwater roots

After heavy rains, river levels in the Amazon can rise by several metres, leading to flooding in large parts of the rainforest. As roots need air to function properly, trees in a flooded forest do not grow as tall as in other areas, as their roots are submerged.

Seeds in water

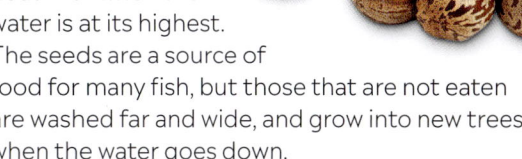

The rubber plant times the release of its seeds – which float – for when the water is at its highest. The seeds are a source of food for many fish, but those that are not eaten are washed far and wide, and grow into new trees when the water goes down.

Near the Atlantic

A woolly spider monkey climbs a vine in the Atlantic Forest on the Brazilian Highlands, near the Atlantic Ocean. A band of hills cuts off this area from the main Amazon Basin. The area is one of the most deforested zones in South America, and many of its animals are endangered.

Floating village
The water body shown here is Lake Titicaca, South America's largest freshwater lake. Nestled nearly 4 km (2.5 miles) above sea level in the Andes, it is inhabited by the Uru people, who live in floating houses made of reeds.

Around the rainforest

The Amazon Basin is surrounded on three sides by mountains. The Guiana Highlands in the north feature incredible waterfalls. To the south are the Brazilian Highlands, a huge mass of rolling hills. To the west lie the Andes – the world's longest mountain range, dotted with volcanoes.

Wall of mountains
The Andes are about 7,000 km (4,350 miles) long, and run from Venezuela in the north to the southern tip of South America. The Central Andes, which run through Ecuador, Peru, and Bolivia, are closest to the Amazon Basin. They contain several high, flat areas, on which ancient civilizations, such as the Incas, once thrived.

Table mountain
At a height of 2,810 m (9,219 ft), Mount Roraima is one of the highest points in the Guiana Highlands. Two billion years old, it is made of a block of sandstone that was left behind after the softer rocks around it were washed away.

Flat summit is covered in rocks and pools of rainwater

EYEWITNESS

Jacques Cousteau
Myths, including stories of a submerged city, surround the magical Lake Titicaca. In 1968, French underwater explorer Jacques Cousteau undertook a six-week investigation of this lake. The expedition was unable to find the lost city but Cousteau discovered animal species new to science, including the Titicaca water frog.

Mountain animals
The high slopes of the Andes Mountains can be very cold and dry. Llamas survive easily there, as they have thick wool. Like their relative, the camel, they can also survive for long periods without water.

Salt flat
Ten cities the size of Paris could fit inside the Salar de Uyuni – the world's largest salt flat. Located in the Bolivian Andes, it was formed when a prehistoric lake dried out, leaving behind a layer of salt. It is also the flattest place on Earth.

Wetlands

Apart from the Amazon River, there are also vast wetlands that collect water in the Amazon Basin. To the south is the Pantanal, the planet's biggest flooded grassland; to the north is Los Llanos, a plain that turns into a huge temporary marshland once a year. These wetlands are fertile and have been important farming regions for centuries. They also contain unique animals, such as the saberfin killifish and the Orinoco crocodile.

Water ways
Water flowing from the hills around the Pantanal collects in a wetland, gets trapped in the basin, and drains away through the Paraguay River. Los Llanos is fed by the yearly flooding of the Orinoco River that covers the low areas of Venezuela and Colombia for months on end.

Giant lily pads
The Victoria lilies of the Pantanal have pads about 2.5 m (8.2 ft) wide, which makes them one of the largest leaves in the world. Although they are fragile, the pads can support the weight of a small child. The lily's large flowers also float on the surface. They are pollinated by beetles that fly from one bloom to the other.

Pink tree
Unlike most forest trees, which are evergreens, the pink lapacho tree is deciduous – it loses its leaves seasonally. It sheds its leaves in the dry, winter months, and grows its flowers before the leaves return in spring. This makes it look pink, and attracts pollinators such as hummingbirds.

Fishing bats

Greater bulldog bats spend their days sleeping in hollow trees or caves. They never move far from water because they have a very unusual diet. These bats use long, curved claws on their rear legs to grab fish close to the surface of the water.

Large feet with claws

Thick tail — *Powerful jaw muscles*
Golden tegu

Golden lizard

The golden tegu is one of the largest lizards in South America, growing to a length of 1 m (3.3 ft). It hunts on land and in water, and can stay underwater for around 20 minutes at a time.

Spear fishing

The anhinga is a fish-hunting water bird that lives in the Pantanal. It spears its prey with its long beak and then swallows the prey whole. Its name means "snakebird" in the local language. When it is in the water, only its long neck and head are visible.

Long, flexible neck

Cattle country

Huge herds of cattle are raised on the Pantanal and Los Llanos. Most of the wetland areas are flooded for only part of the year, so when the water recedes, lush pastures grow on the fertile soil. Cowboys – known as *Pantaneiros* in the Pantanal and *Llaneros* in Los Llanos – look after the cattle herds in these areas. Cattle-ranching forms the economic backbone of the Pantanal and Los Llanos.

Plants and fungi

Plant ponds
This poison dart frog raises its tadpole in a small pond that has formed in the base of a bromeliad plant. Bromeliads have fleshy leaves, which fan out in a circle creating a bowl shape.

The Amazon Rainforest is a complex community of plants that are communicating all the time beneath the ground via a network of fine fungal threads. About a third of the rainforest plants are trees. The rest include rootless plants that take water from the air, vines, and even species that catch insects. This region also teems with fungi, many of which turn dead leaves into food for the forest.

Sticky liquid on soft stalks

Moth stuck to leaf

Strangler fig
This network of stems (above) once contained a tree trunk. The stems belong to a strangler fig, a plant that grows from a seed at the top of a tall tree. The roots grow down to the ground to get water and nutrients and encircle the tree trunk. Eventually, the tree inside dies under the weight of the fig and rots away.

Eating bugs
Sundews live in swampy regions of the rainforest. Their leaves are covered in soft stalks, coated in a sticky liquid. When an insect lands on the leaf, it becomes stuck. The leaf then curls around the insect and digests it, extracting any useful nutrients.

WOOD WIDE WEB

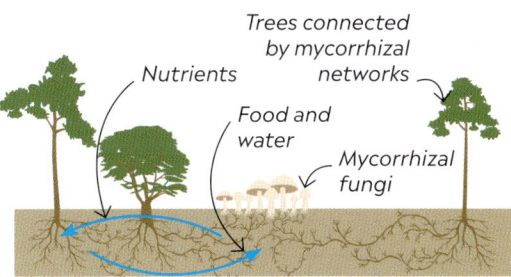

Nutrients — *Trees connected by mycorrhizal networks* — *Food and water* — *Mycorrhizal fungi*

Beneath the forest floor, there is a thriving network of roots and fungi called the "mycorrhizal" (fungal) network. This "social" network connects trees and plants to each other, and enables them to share nutrients and information – a kind of "wood wide web" for trees. In return, the fungi get water and food from the trees.

Giant trees called kapok have buttress roots – wide roots that grow from high on a tree trunk to support it.

Cecropia ant carrying oily nodule produced by plant

Symbiosis

Cecropia trees recruit an army of ants to defend them against attack. The ants live in hollow spaces in the trees, cleaning fungus off the leaves and attacking other insects that venture onto the plant. As a reward, the plant produces oily nodules, which the ants cut off and eat. This relationship – in which both the plant and animal benefit – is called symbiosis.

Up in the air

About a quarter of rainforest plants do not grow a long stem or trunk to reach sunlight. Instead, they grow on bigger plants above the ground. These plants – known as epiphytes – have leaves, flowers, and fruits, but no true roots. They get the water they need from the moisture in the air.

Spores fall out of the cap as the tiny, cup-shaped mushroom dries out.

Forest mushrooms

Fungi are key waste recyclers in the forest. These mushrooms (right) are growing on and inside the dead wood, helping it to rot away and release nutrients into the soil.

19

Birds of the Amazon

Green-billed toucan

Long bill
The toucan's long, chunky bill makes up about a quarter of its body length. Its bill has rough edges that are useful for cracking nuts and peeling fruits. Toucans rarely fly far, preferring to hop from branch to branch.

Around 1,500 bird species live in the Amazon Rainforest. They range from macaws – the world's biggest parrots – to tiny hummingbirds. Many water birds also live in the region's vast wetlands and along its riverbanks. Forest birds have plenty of places to hide, but the males can use their colourful plumage when they want to be seen, especially when they want to attract mates.

> A toucan's bill is made of a spongy bone covered in **a coat of keratin**, the material found in human fingernails.

Hovering to feed
Although it weighs only 9 g (0.3 oz) and is just 15 cm (6 in) long, the swallowtail hummingbird is the largest hummingbird in the Amazon. Its wings beat at a rate of 50 times a second, allowing it to hover in front of a flower while sipping the nectar with its tongue.

High fliers
Macaws eat unripe fruits that most forest animals ignore, as the bird's hooked beak can rip away the tough outer layers of the fruits. They also often gather in large flocks on muddy riverbanks, where they lick the soil to get the salts and nutrients missing in their food.

Laughing falcon
This bird of prey with a high-pitched cackle perches above a clearing and looks for prey on the ground. When it spots a victim, such as a snake, it swoops down and lands on top of it. It kills its victims with a quick bite to the back of the head.

Coral snake

Hanging nests
These bags of woven grasses and twigs are the nests of green oropendolas – songbirds that eat insects and fruits. Each nest cluster is a breeding colony ruled by a single male, who mates with most of the females there. Each female lays two eggs at the bottom of a nest.

Bright plumage

The tail makes up more than half the bird's length.

White bill with black tip

Large, circular eyes

Colourful songbird
Feeding on insects, paradise tanagers are little songbirds that live in the forest canopy. The males are brightly coloured so that they can get noticed by mates. The females build small, cup-shaped nests hidden among the leaves.

Fishing for food
The boat-billed heron is a water bird that uses its long legs to wade through shallow water. It scoops up food using its wide, shovel-shaped bill, which helps it to feel for prey in the mud. The heron shown here is about to feast on a fish, but this species also eats shellfish and birds' eggs.

Adults have a crest of spiked feathers.

👁 EYEWITNESS

Gonzalo Cardona Molina
Colombian conservationist Gonzalo Cardona Molina saved the yellow-eared parrot from extinction. Between 1998 and 2020, he protected the birds' habitat and ran awareness programmes. The parrot's numbers have grown from 80 to more than 3,800.

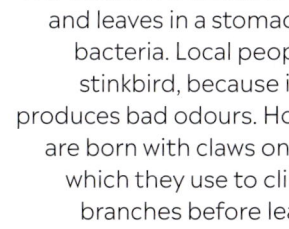

Stinkbird
The hoatzin ferments meals of fruits and leaves in a stomach filled with bacteria. Local people call it the stinkbird, because its digestion produces bad odours. Hoatzin chicks are born with claws on their wings, which they use to climb through branches before learning to fly.

21

Amazon monkeys

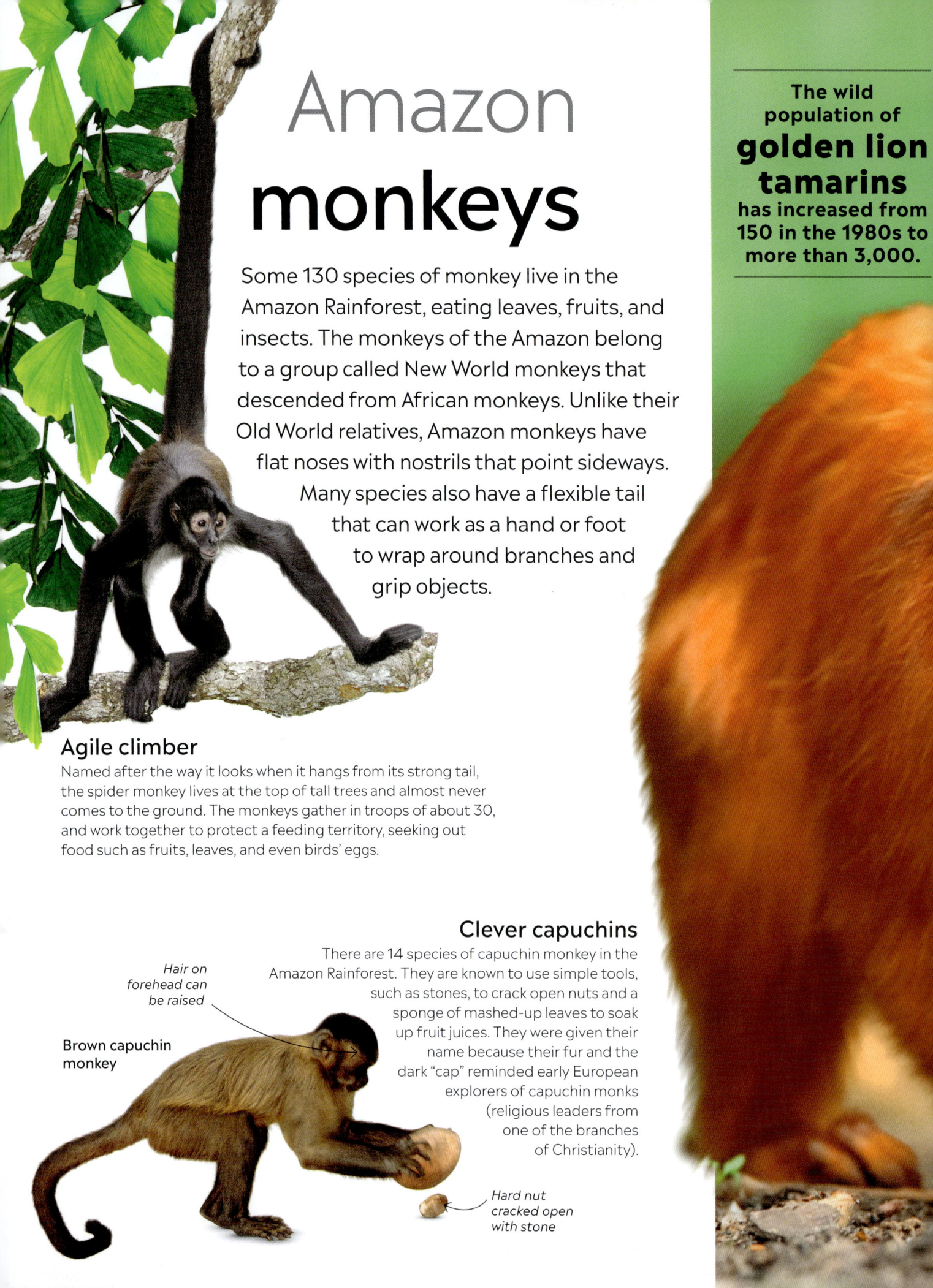

Some 130 species of monkey live in the Amazon Rainforest, eating leaves, fruits, and insects. The monkeys of the Amazon belong to a group called New World monkeys that descended from African monkeys. Unlike their Old World relatives, Amazon monkeys have flat noses with nostrils that point sideways. Many species also have a flexible tail that can work as a hand or foot to wrap around branches and grip objects.

The wild population of **golden lion tamarins** has increased from 150 in the 1980s to more than 3,000.

Agile climber
Named after the way it looks when it hangs from its strong tail, the spider monkey lives at the top of tall trees and almost never comes to the ground. The monkeys gather in troops of about 30, and work together to protect a feeding territory, seeking out food such as fruits, leaves, and even birds' eggs.

Clever capuchins
There are 14 species of capuchin monkey in the Amazon Rainforest. They are known to use simple tools, such as stones, to crack open nuts and a sponge of mashed-up leaves to soak up fruit juices. They were given their name because their fur and the dark "cap" reminded early European explorers of capuchin monks (religious leaders from one of the branches of Christianity).

Hair on forehead can be raised

Brown capuchin monkey

Hard nut cracked open with stone

Lion's mane

The flowing mane of a golden lion tamarin resembles the mane of a lion. These brightly coloured monkeys live in the dense, hot, and humid jungles of the Atlantic Forest. They are most active in the cool mornings and evenings, and take a nap during the middle of the day. Only the chief male and female breed.

Howler monkeys can grow up to 90 cm (35 in) tall.

Loud howler

Howler monkeys are not only the largest and noisiest monkeys in the Amazon Rainforest, but also the loudest land animals. Their calls can travel up to 4 km (2.5 miles) through the forest. They use their large, flexible throats to boost their volume when calling from the treetops.

Hairless face

Adult marmosets are only 12 cm (4.7 in) long.

Large eyes see only in black and white.

Mini monkey

The pygmy marmoset is the tiniest monkey in the world. It lives in small bushes that grow along riverbanks and the edge of the forest. Its main food is sap – a sweet, sticky liquid produced by plants.

Nocturnal monkey

The douroucoulis, or owl monkeys, are the only monkey species in the world that is nocturnal, or active at night. Their huge eyes allow them to see well enough in the dark to run and jump through the branches. They move around in small family groups.

On the forest floor

Flatworm
Most of the world's flatworms live in water, but it is so humid in the Amazon Rainforest that some, such as the Amazonian land planarian (above), slither around on the ground. If it is bitten in half by a predator, a new worm will grow back from each half.

Not all animals in the Amazon Rainforest live in trees – many species, including the giant armadillo and the peccary, also live on the forest floor. The thick covering of trees means very little sunlight reaches the ground. There is not much wind down there either, and the moisture in the air makes it very humid.

Circles of pale fur around eyes look like spectacles.

Tough, dark brown shell composed of bony plates

Giant armadillo
The Amazon's giant armadillo – the world's largest species of armadillo – can grow up to 1.5 m (5 ft) long. This forest giant forages at night and digs its way into termite mounds and ant nests using long claws on its forelegs. It licks up the insects inside using a long, sticky tongue.

Pack hunters
Bush dogs are related to wolves. They work in packs of around 12 to chase rodents and ground birds through the forest. They make squeaking calls to keep track of each other.

Spectacled bear
The spectacled bear is the only bear species in the Amazon Rainforest. It is not a fierce hunter. During the day, it prefers to sleep in a cave or hollow tree. At night, it climbs through low branches, feeding on fruits, lush leaves, and any insects and rodents it can catch.

Long claws help to grip while climbing.

24

A flexible snout helps to sniff out food, water, and mates.

Arrow-shaped head gives the snake its name.

Deadly viper
The lancehead is a venomous viper that lies hidden among fallen leaves and strikes when prey, such as a rodent, walks past. Its venom does not kill straight away. If its prey escapes, the snake tracks its victim using heat-sensitive pits on its snout.

Gentle giants
Weighing more than three adult humans put together, tapirs are the largest animals in the Amazon. They feed on leaves, grass, and fruit. Baby tapirs are striped, which helps them hide inside the shadows of the forest.

Jungle cat
The ocelot may look like a leopard, but it is not much bigger than a domestic cat. During the day it sleeps on a shady branch, but at night it hunts, mostly on the ground, tracking small prey, such as opossums, mice, and frogs, by their smell. It has excellent night vision.

Creepy crawlies

Insects, spiders, worms, and other invertebrates make up almost 95 per cent of all animal species in the Amazon Rainforest. One survey confirmed that about 50,000 insect species live in every 2.59 sq km (1 sq mile) of the rainforest. Scientists have also calculated that ants, wasps, and termites equal more than half of the total weight of animals in the Amazon. So, put together, they far outweigh all the big vertebrates, such as mammals, birds, and reptiles.

Hard-working ants
An army ant colony of more than a million ants spreads out in a column 100 m (330 ft) long. Ants make up 30 per cent of the Amazon Rainforest biomass, and have a diet that includes insects, snakes, frogs, and birds. The ant workers use their bodies to make a bridge over an obstacle, as seen here.

Startling cricket
A katydid is a type of cricket: this one (right) is known as a peacock katydid. It has a green body, and its wings look like a drying leaf. If a predator were to spot it, this insect might open its wings wide like a peacock to reveal bright "eyespots" to startle the attacker.

Eyespot on wing

Titan beetle

Fungus beetle

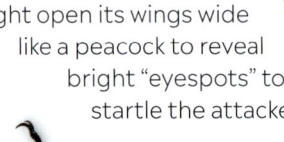
Hercules beetle

Beetle mania
Beetles are one of the most common types of insect, and the Amazon Rainforest has more than its fair share of them. It is home to the titan beetle, which is 16 cm (6.3 in) long and has mouthparts strong enough to cut through a pencil. At up to 17 cm (6.7 in), the Hercules beetle is even longer.

Monster centipede
The Amazon giant centipede is one of the largest centipedes in the world. At about 25 cm (9.8 in) long, it hunts all over the rainforest, using its 36 or more clawed feet to climb in the trees. With its powerful venom, it preys on many animals, including snakes and birds.

Winged beauty
The Amazon Rainforest has at least 2,000 butterfly species, the most vibrant of which are the shimmering morphos. An owl butterfly tries to stay hidden, but if a predator closes in, the big butterfly opens its wings to show two large eyespots that make it look like the face of a scary owl.

Owl butterfly

Blue morpho butterfly

Vein pattern similar to that of a leaf

Mimic
The thorax (mid-body) of the praying mantis looks more like a plant than an insect. This helps the mantis stay hidden from predators, such as frogs and birds, and also makes the insect invisible to its prey.

Hind wings resemble folded leaves.

Flying spider
Selenops spiders spend their lives in the treetops. When threatened by a predator, they jump into the air. Their flat bodies allow them to gently float down to another branch like a falling feather instead of crashing to the forest floor. They can even steer themselves in flight and choose where to land.

Jumping spider

Goliath bird-eating spider

Eight-legged giant
The Amazon's Goliath bird-eating spider is as large as a dinner plate, but it mainly eats earthworms. The region is also home to the tiny jumping spider, which, amazingly, can jump 30 times its own body length.

27

In and around the river

Several animals that are more common in the ocean have made their home in the rivers of the Amazon Basin. For example, there are dolphins living in the flooded forests of Peru and Ecuador, 3,000 km (1,864 miles) from the ocean. Some animals also live on the riverbanks, including capybaras, which are semiaquatic rodents.

River dolphins have long beaks.

River dolphin
The Amazon river dolphin, or boto, spends most of the year in the wide, deep rivers. In the rainy season, the rivers flood parts of the forest, and the dolphins follow the water to feed among the tree trunks.

> **EYEWITNESS**
>
>
>
> **Fernando Trujillo**
> Born in Colombia, Fernando Trujillo spent his childhood exploring the Amazon Rainforest rivers and grew fascinated with the endangered pink dolphins. Trujillo set up the Omacha Foundation, a conservation group dedicated to saving dolphins and other Amazonian species.

River mermaid
The Amazonian manatee looks like a seal, but it is an aquatic relative of the elephant. Some manatees – although not this species – live out in the ocean, and legend has it that lonely sailors mistook them for mermaids.

A barrel-shaped body contains a large gut that is ideal for digesting plants.

Eyes on top of the head help the capybara to stay alert even when it is almost completely submerged in water.

Feet are partially webbed, which helps when swimming.

Thick fur keeps out water.

Huge rodent

The order of animals known as rodents includes small creatures such as mice and squirrels. At 1.3 m (4.3 ft) long and weighing as much as an adult human, the capybara is the world's largest rodent. Its sharp front teeth can slice through plant stems. Capybaras live in herds that graze together on the lush riverbank.

Giant otter

Measuring up to 1.4 m (4.6 ft) long, the Amazonian giant otter is the largest otter in the world. Large, webbed feet and a long, flattened tail make it a very powerful swimmer. Because it is not agile on land, this species seldom ventures far from the riverbank.

Fine, dense, water-repellent fur

Yapok

A relative of Australia's kangaroos and koalas, the yapok is an aquatic marsupial – a mammal that carries its babies in a pouch and which spends much of its time in the water. The yapok's pouch is watertight, so the young do not drown.

Flippers help the Amazonian manatee to steer in the water.

29

Hunting for food

Front legs are raised during an attack.

The Amazon Rainforest teems with deadly hunters – on the ground, in the water, and in the treetops. They include not only big cats, massive caiman, and giant snakes, but also the world's deadliest spiders, birds big enough to kill monkeys, a 2-m- (6.5-ft-) long fish that can give an electric shock, and a bat that drinks blood.

Deadly hunter
Although most spiders are harmless to humans, the Brazilian wandering spider is one of the most dangerous spiders on Earth. In the absence of treatment, its venom could kill a person in 30 minutes. This deadly spider chases mice on the forest floor or frogs among the leaves, killing them in seconds with a single bite.

Bloodsucker
The vampire bat comes out to feed on dark, moonless nights. It lands near sleeping mammals, including humans, and crawls over their bodies searching for a warm patch of skin. It then makes a tiny cut with its pointed fangs and drinks the blood that flows out.

The flat snout is used to feel for warm skin.

Giant snake
At up to 5 m (16.4 ft) long, the green anaconda – one of the world's largest snakes – spends most of its time in shallow water, ready to ambush prey that wanders too close to the water's edge. The anaconda shown here has captured a caiman – another fearsome predator. The snake kills its victim by squeezing it so tightly that it stops breathing. Like all snakes, it swallows its prey whole.

Night stalker
The jaguar is the Amazon Rainforest's largest land predator, and is usually a lone, nocturnal hunter. It leaps on its prey, such as tapirs and caimans, from above, killing them with a skull-crushing bite. By day, the jaguar snoozes on a shaded branch. The fur's pattern helps the big cat blend in to its environment.

2-m- (6.5-ft-) wide wingspan

On the wing
The harpy eagle is the largest bird of prey in the Amazon Rainforest. It perches high up in the forest, and when it spots its prey, it swoops down and grabs its victim with its huge talons. This eagle often captures monkeys, killing them with a bite from its hooked beak, and carries them back to its perch to eat. It also dives to the forest floor to grab ground mammals, and plucks smaller birds out of the air.

Killer caiman
The Amazon Rainforest's caiman (a type of alligator) can grow up to 6 m (19.6 ft) long. They lie in shallow water and when land animals come too close, they pull them under the water and drown them. They will also attack fish and birds on the water's surface.

Short, stocky legs are good for swimming and climbing.

Horn-like projections above the eyes

Of both worlds

Frogs, toads, and salamanders are amphibians – animals that live in water and on land. Yet, most amphibians cannot survive for long without water, which is abundant in the Amazon Rainforest. A huge range of amphibians thrive there – from worm-like creatures that burrow through damp soil, to frogs that are poisonous to touch.

Big mouth
One of the Amazon Rainforest's largest amphibians, the horned frog can grow up to 20 cm (8 in) long. This frog hides itself in leaves, then uses its huge mouth, measuring half the size of its body, to gulp down mice, lizards, and other frogs.

See-through
The glass frog's upper body looks green, but its belly skin has no colour, making its heart, stomach, and bones visible. It sleeps on leaves, and because its skin is transparent, the colour of the leaf filters through, making the frog hard to spot.

Unusual toad
The Surinam toad lives in water. It uses its long, sensitive fingers to find fish and other prey in the riverbed. During mating, the male loads fertilized eggs onto the female's back, where they are absorbed into the skin. Tiny toadlets hatch from the eggs and burst out of the mother's back.

Eggs on the back of the female toad

Paradoxical frog
A paradox is something that seems impossible but is true. This Amazonian frog is a paradox because its tadpole, which grows up to 22 cm (9 in) long, gets smaller as it gets older. When it is an adult frog, it is a third of that size.

Pretty poisonous
Poison dart frogs get their name because Amazonian hunters used the powerful toxins in the skin of the species to make poisoned darts for killing monkeys. These toxins come from the chemicals in ants and other insects that these frogs eat. The brightly coloured skin serves as a warning to predators to stay away.

Red poison dart frog

Yellow poison arrow frog

Blue poison dart frog

EYEWITNESS

Marcy Sieggreen
An expert in Amazonian frogs, US scientist Marcy Sieggreen set up the "Amazon Amphibian Protectors Club" in schools in Peru in 2012. She helped students monitor frog populations and taught them to breed frogs in captivity before releasing them in the wild.

During the breeding season, the male tree frog shakes small branches to attract the female.

Tree dweller
The red-eyed tree frog has long, slender legs for climbing and jumping, and its fingers and toes have round suction cups for gripping branches. Like other tree frogs, it lays its eggs on leaves overhanging a pool. When the tadpoles hatch, they fall into the water beneath.

Large eyes help the frog to see at night

Bright coloration startles predators

The tree frog's skin releases a bad-tasting slime that deters predators.

Limbless
Although it resembles a worm or snake, this creature is a type of caecilian – a limbless amphibian that burrows through soil and eats underground insects. Caecilian babies feed on their mother's skin, pausing occasionally to let it grow back.

Salamander
The Amazon Rainforest's salamanders (above) have webbed feet to grip leaves and branches. Most active at night, they catch insects with their long, sticky tongues. They lack lungs and do not breathe air; instead, they absorb oxygen through their moist skin.

Suction pads on fingers help the frog to climb.

The pointed snout pushes through soil.

Green and black poison dart frog | Amazon dart frog | Pasco poison dart frog | Imitating poison frog

Forest reptiles

Reptiles have scaly skin and live in the warmer parts of the world. From killer crocodiles to venomous snakes, around 500 reptile species live in many places in the Amazon Rainforest, including the treetops and the deepest rivers. However, there are probably many more that scientists are yet to discover.

Warning flap
This tree-climbing anole lizard has a skin flap on its neck called a dewlap. When a predator comes too close, the lizard unfurls the flap, scaring off the predator. Males have a brighter dewlap than females, and they often flash it in and out to attract mates.

Heat-sensitive pits are located along upper and lower lips.

Sensing heat
The bright green body of the emerald tree boa helps it to blend in with the leaves. At night it hunts for mice, using heat-sensitive pits on its snout to track prey in the dark. These pits sense body heat given off by other animals.

Males have longer spikes than females.

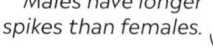

Jungle dragon
Also known as a wood lizard, the forest dragon has a ridge of armoured spikes along its back and tail. If threatened, it opens its mouth in a wide gape, revealing bright pink gums. The sudden flash of colour often startles any attacker, and helps the lizard to escape.

Tiny caiman
Seen here is a baby dwarf caiman. Among all crocodiles and alligators, Cuvier's dwarf caimans are the world's smallest, growing to little more than 1.6 m (5.3 ft) in length. They live in small streams and hunt for water snails, crabs, and frogs.

Targeting prey

The long and slender vine snake slithers through branches to reach out and grab lizards, chicks, and other prey. Unlike most other snakes, this venomous species is able to swivel its eyeballs, which helps it to spot and target its prey before a strike.

Giant turtle

The male Arrau turtle is the Amazon Rainforest's largest turtle, growing up to 1 m (3.3 ft) long. Females bury their eggs on sandbars that are exposed in the dry season, when the water level drops. The baby turtles hatch at the start of the rainy season.

Bulge on head contains venom glands

Triangular head shape

Ambush hunter

The eyelash viper's scales break up the shape of the snake's face, so it can hide from its prey among the leaves. The 60-cm- (24-in-) long viper wiggles the point of its tail to attract curious birds and lizards. It then ambushes them, delivering a venomous bite at lightning speed.

Amazon fish

The many rivers found in the Amazon Basin are home to nearly 3,000 species of fish – 10 per cent of all the world's fish species. The water in some places does not contain much oxygen, especially when the river levels are low. As a result, even though they all have gills, some Amazon fish are able to breathe air as well.

Feeding frenzy

A piranha only grows to about 20 cm (7.8 in) long, but this sharp-toothed fish has a fearsome reputation. It is said that these fish can devour large animals, including cattle and humans, within minutes. However, these attacks are rare, and they only occur when the river level is low and the piranhas are trapped in shallow water. Most piranhas eat other fish, while some species are vegetarian.

Venomous sting

Rays, such as this stingray, are related to sharks, and the Amazon River is home to more than 20 species of them. Known as the ocellate river stingray, this fish defends itself with a venomous spike in its tail. However, it does not use its tail to catch prey, which includes crustaceans and snails.

Giant fish

The arapaima is the largest freshwater fish in the world, weighing up to 200 kg (440 lb). The longest specimen ever caught was 4.25 m (15 ft) long, but most are about half that length. This giant fish has gills, but it also breathes air using a lung-like organ, taking a gulp of air every 10 minutes or so.

Deadly shark

At 3 m (9.8 ft) long, the bull shark is one of the largest sharks in the world. Known for its aggressive nature, this predator specializes in hunting in shallow, muddy, coastal water. They have been spotted 4,000 km (2,485 miles) upstream on the Amazon River.

The bull shark has at least 350 teeth.

Male arowanas hold the females' **fertilized eggs** in their mouth until they hatch.

EYEWITNESS

Lesley de Souza
Brazilian conservation biologist Dr Lesley de Souza specializes in Amazonian fish. She discovered six new species of catfish in 2019. She is also working with Indigenous communities in the Amazon to conserve the arapaima.

Distinctive metallic blue and orange stripe

Water monkey

The arowana feeds mainly on fish. However, it can also leap up to 2 m (6.5 ft) out of the water to snatch birds, bugs, or other prey. Because of this unique behaviour, locals refer to this species as the "water monkey".

Tetras

Just 2 cm (0.8 in) long, neon tetras are bright little freshwater fish found commonly in home aquaria all over the world. However, their natural habitat is in the Amazon River. The first pet tetras were taken from this river in the 1930s. They are bred in captivity today, with nearly 20 million being sold every year in the United States alone.

Ancient civilizations

People have lived in the Amazon region for at least 12,500 years. For a long time, scientists thought the region was an untouched wilderness, but new evidence shows that large settlements existed even in the densest parts of the jungle. The civilizations that grew up around the edge of the rainforest are the most well known. They included the mighty Inca Empire of the Andes.

Marajoara pottery
This jar contained the ashes of a person who died about 1,000 years ago, and was made by the Marajoara people. They are named after Marajó Island, which, located at the Amazon River's mouth, was the centre of their civilization. Much of what is known about them comes from their pottery.

Buildings made from stone blocks

EYEWITNESS

Denise Schaan
Brazilian archaeologist Dr Denise Schaan studied the ancient history of the Amazon Rainforest using satellite photographs. She noticed marks on the ground that were evidence of buildings, walls, and even paths in ancient villages – showing that people lived here around 2,000 years ago.

Ancient rock paintings

Hidden in the Colombian forest are some of the world's most historically significant rock paintings. Many of these are around 12,500 years old, and were created by some of the first humans to live in the Amazon. There are images showing people, intricate patterns, and extinct ice-age animals, such as giant sloths and mastodons.

Cliff burial

This 500-year-old mummy was buried in a cave carved into a cliff in the Peruvian Andes. This person was a member of the Chachapoya people, who flourished from around 800 CE, and lived high in the mountains. Several mummies have been preserved by the cold, dry air, often buried in cliffside tombs. The high mountain forests are called cloud forests, and the people who lived there were called Warriors of the Clouds.

Earrings represent a chief figure

Hammered and flattened pure gold

Made of gold

The Muisca people, who lived in the mountains of Colombia between 600 and 1600 CE, made this gold figure. In one ritual, a Muiscal chief was covered in gold dust, which he washed off in a sacred mountain lake. Priests threw other gold artefacts into the lake as gifts to the goddess who was believed to live there. These rituals would eventually give rise to the myth of *El Dorado*, the legendary kingdom of gold.

The great Inca

Machu Picchu, seen below in ruins, is a city built by the powerful, ancient Inca Empire in the Andes, about 250 km (155 miles) north of the Amazon River's source. It was built around 1450 as a retreat for the Inca emperor Pachauti.

Ciudad Perdida

The Ciudad Perdida, or "lost city" – located on the northernmost tip of the Andes range in Colombia – lay forgotten until the 1970s. Nobody knows who built it, but archaeologists think it is around 1,400 years old. The city has terraced fields and paved roads. Nearly 5,000 people may have lived there.

Exploration and exploitation

Millions of people lived in the Amazon before Europeans arrived. In 1494, European colonial powers Spain and Portugal planned to take over this land and agreed to divide what they believed to be the "new world" by drawing a vertical line between the Americas and Europe. This line went right through the Amazon Basin. A Spanish army conquered the Inca Empire, to the west of the line, creating the territory of Peru, while the Portuguese settled at the mouth of the Amazon River, to the east, eventually creating Brazil.

Amazons
In 1542, Spanish conquistador Francisco de Orellana travelled all the way down the Amazon River to the ocean. His men were attacked by female warriors – known as Amazons in Greek mythology – and he gave their name to the river.

Enslaved labour
The European colonists enslaved Indigenous peoples to work in the Amazon region's mines and plantations. Thousands of Indigenous peoples died from overwork and from diseases brought by the Europeans. The colonists also forcibly transported enslaved Africans to the area. Between 1550 and 1880, around 6 million Africans were forced to labour in harsh conditions here.

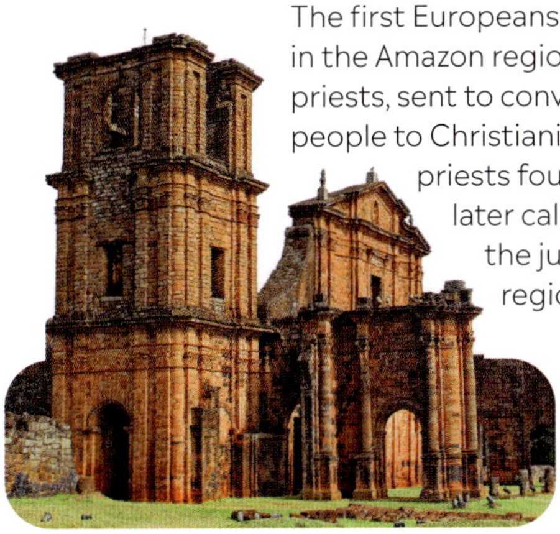

A new religion
The first Europeans to travel in the Amazon region included Jesuit priests, sent to convert the local people to Christianity. Some of these priests founded churches – later called missions – in the jungle. Many of the region's first modern towns grew around these sites.

Rubber boom
In the 1880s, the Amazon region became the world centre for rubber production – this period became known as the "Rubber Boom". Ruthless business people took over large areas of rainforest, enslaved the local people, and forced them to work day and night. The rubber boom ended 30 years later because rubber had begun to be produced in other parts of the world.

Statue of Pedro Teixeira in Belém, Brazil, where his journey began

Upstream explorer
In 1637, Portuguese colonist Pedro Teixeira led 47 canoes – carrying 70 Portuguese soldiers as well as 1,200 Indigenous Amazon peoples and African slaves – upstream from the mouth of the Amazon River to present-day Ecuador. They wanted to know how far east Spanish conquerors had advanced. These men claimed the valley for Portugal.

Cinnamon sticks are pieces of bark from the cinnamon tree.

The long snout grabs slippery fish.

Seeking cinnamon
Early European conquerers were looking for spices, which were very valuable in the 16th century. In 1541, Spanish conquistador Gonzalo Pizarro heard about a Valley of Cinnamon located to the east of the Andes. He went looking for it, in the hope of becoming wealthy, but returned empty handed.

Explorers' species
Many of the Amazon's animals are named after naturalists and scientists who led expeditions into the rainforest. For example, the Amazon river dolphin (right), *Inia geoffrensis*, was named after the French researcher Étienne Geoffroy Saint-Hilaire; Isabel's saki, *Pithecia isabela*, was named after Isabel Godin des Odonais of Peru, who crossed the Amazon in 1728.

Myths

The Amazon Rainforest is home to many myths and legends. Some ancient stories revolve around good and evil forest spirits, while other myths arose around the time the first Europeans reached the rainforest. Many European colonizers heard stories about lost cities and treasures. They never found anything, but the legends lived on, adding more mystique to this incredible region.

Phantom boa

In the rainforest's western parts, many Indigenous peoples believe in the legend of Sachamama, the "spirit mother" of the jungle who looks like a huge snake. People often mistake her body for a fallen tree trunk. Sachamama is considered to be a kind spirit, but will rise up and eat any person who steps on her.

Armoured scales on fish

Banished fish

Legend has it that the arapaima (also called pirarucu), the Amazon's biggest fish, is a warrior banished by the gods. The warrior, Pirarucu, was cruel to the villagers, so the gods taught him a lesson. On a stormy fishing trip, Pirarucu was too proud to seek shelter, so was struck by lightning, which turned him into the fish.

42

Sacred cassava

The cassava root – known as mandioca to the people of the Amazon Rainforest – is thought to be a gift from the gods. Legend has it that a chief's unmarried daughter was made pregnant by the gods. She gave birth to a pale-skinned girl called Mani. Sadly, Mani died on her first birthday, and a strange new plant grew from her grave. This plant was the delicious mandioca.

Postage stamp from Brazil showing the mandioca legend

Quest for gold

Gold was common in the Andes, and the Inca and other Indigenous peoples made many objects from it, such as this mask from Colombia. Many European conquerors came to the Americas hoping to find the city of *El Dorado* – literally "the golden one". However, no one could find this mythical kingdom.

Young lupuna tree

Sorcerer tree

Many Amazon villages regard the largest and oldest lupuna tree in the area as a "sorcerer tree". It is believed that the tree can punish bad people by giving them a terrible stomach ache. Some people leave the possessions of their enemies at the base of the trunk, in the hope that the tree will make them suffer.

Lost city of the Inca

In the 16th century, after the Spanish conquered the Inca Empire, the Inca fled their cities. But a rumour spread that an army moved to a hidden city called Vilcabamba. Many lost Inca towns have been rediscovered since, such as Huinay Huayna (below) in 1941. However, no one has been able to identify Vilcabamba yet.

Velvety wings absorb sound and allow the owl to fly silently.

Owl spirit

The Amazon Rainforest's owls are said to embody the spirit of the moon goddess Chia. According to an ancient myth, the god of farming, Chibchacum, turned Chia into an owl because she made people very lazy and badly behaved.

Stone walls have survived erosion.

Traditional life

Millions of people lived in the Amazon region before the Europeans arrived in the 16th century. There are about a million Indigenous Amazonians left today, although some tribes only have a few hundred members. Many follow the ways of their ancestors, gathering everything they need from the forest.

Secluded tribes

This Indigenous man belongs to the Matis tribe that lives in the far west of the Amazon region. The tribe first made contact with Brazilian government officials in 1978. The Matis had no natural defences against diseases common in the rest of the world and about 80 per cent of them died from viral infections caught from outsiders. Originally semi-nomadic, the Matis tribe now lives in two villages.

Arrows used to shoot monkeys in trees

New bows are crafted every few months by hunters as wood rots quickly in the damp rainforest.

Spirituality in medicine

A shaman is a spiritual leader and healer of the sick. Anyone who falls sick is taken to a shaman for herbal medicines made from forest plants and for rituals believed to help in healing. Men and women can be shamans.

The Amazon's Indigenous peoples use more than 2,000 different plants as medicines.

Hunting and gathering

A group of hunters show their skill with long bows made from wood cut from forest trees. The men belong to the Awá tribe, one of the smallest communities living in the rainforest. They move regularly to new camps, where the women gather food, catch fish, and prepare meals. Only around 10 per cent of their diet comes from hunting.

Body painted with natural dyes

River food

The Amazon River and its tributaries are an important source of food for the local people. These fishermen are from the Yawalapiti tribe living along the Xingu River. They catch fish by spearing them using bows and arrows.

Following rituals

Young Amazonian people often participate in ancient ceremonies. Every year, the tribes of the Xingu area, located in the south-eastern part of the Amazon region, gather for a festival. The tribes organize dances, rituals, and other events.

Leg bindings strengthen ankles for wrestling.

Traditional craft

The Amazon region's Indigenous peoples know how to make everything they need from materials found in the forest. This woman from the Yanomami tribe, which lives on the border of Venezuela and Brazil, is making a basket from natural fibres.

Modern Amazonia

Beach resort
The Amazon region has a beach resort 1,450 km (901 miles) away from the ocean. Located at Ponta Negra – on the edge of Manaus, Brazil – bathers take a dip in the Rio Negro, home to Amazon river dolphins and many fish. Lifeguards keep watch over the swimmers, but also look out for caimans (a type of alligator).

In big cities, such as Manaus in Brazil, modern buildings stand next to traditional homes. Yet even here, you are never more than 10 km (6.2 miles) from the rainforest, and riverboats are often the best way to travel between towns and cities.

One village may have more than a hundred solar panels.

Amazon communication
Many rainforests grow in very sunny places – and these solar panels are using that sunlight to supply electricity for a village in the Amazon Rainforest. The electricity powers computers and charges mobile phones. Telecommunication masts on the riverbanks transmit telephone calls and Internet signals. Social media is hugely popular with young people.

This medical boat belongs to the Peruvian navy.

Floating hospital
It can take a long time to get to a hospital in remote parts of the Amazon Rainforest. Hospital ships (above) make regular visits to isolated villages so that those in need can receive treatment. In emergencies, faster river ambulances take patients to the nearest city hospital.

River village

Most Amazonian villages are built beside the river. Houses are placed high on the riverbank so they do not flood when water levels are high. Seen here is a floating village called Belén in Iquitos, Peru. The houses – attached to poles driven into the riverbed – float on the river itself, rising and falling with the water.

Roof thatched with dried palm leaves

Carnival culture

These jaguar dancers are performing at a carnival in Parintins, a Brazilian city located beside the Amazon River. A carnival is a party that can be enjoyed by thousands of people from all around the world over several days. Big cities in Brazil have a strong tradition of carnivals, merging African and European traditions with Indigenous Amazonian culture.

Plumed headdress

Soccer city

The Arena da Amazônia stadium was built for the 2014 FIFA World Cup. Its design was inspired by the straw baskets woven by people in the region. Manaus is hot and humid, so the stadium's ventilation system, shaded areas, and its structure help to keep the spectators reasonably comfortable.

Schooling

Instead of attending formal schooling, many children in Amazonian villages grow up learning the skills they need to survive in the forest. For those who later move towards cities, it can be difficult to get by without reading and writing skills. Government initiatives are now helping to build schools and bring literacy skills to more rural areas.

Getting around

The land is heavily forested in the Amazon region, so the long, wide rivers are ideal for travelling long distances. Even though modern highways now cut through the rainforest, and aircraft connect remote villages with the rest of the world, many of the people living in this region get around by boat, just as they have done for thousands of years.

On the road
In the 1970s, the Brazilian government cut a 5,000-km (3,100-mile) roadway from the Atlantic Coast through the Amazon Rainforest to the border with Peru. This Trans-Amazonian Highway is still unfinished, but it has allowed road traffic, and even loggers, right into the heart of the rainforest.

Bridges
The only road bridge in the Amazon river system crosses the Rio Negro near the city of Manaus, Brazil. Opened in 2011 and 3,595 m (11,800 ft) long, it had to be high enough for ocean-going cargo ships and the Amazon's ferries to travel to Manaus's port – the region's main transport hub.

Just walk!
Away from the river, the only way to travel through the jungle is by foot. Even the toughest off-road vehicles cannot make their way through the undergrowth and fallen trees. The tourists seen here are taking a short stroll. For longer journeys, travellers need to have a machete to cut through bushes that block their way. Tourism is a big industry in the Amazon Rainforest.

Riding on horseback

Sure-footed horses and mules are the best way to travel in the foothills of the Andes. Before horses were brought to the region by 16th-century European explorers, Andean people used llamas to carry cargo. However, llamas are not strong enough to carry humans.

Llamas can carry loads as heavy as 25 per cent of their body weight.

Air travel

The calm waters of the Amazon River make a good runway for seaplanes. The largest Amazonian cities, such as Manaus and Iquitos, have full-sized airports, but small aircraft, as shown, can fly to remote communities far from any city. Inland, away from the river, skilled pilots land planes on airstrips cut from the forest.

The float allows the plane to land on water.

Going for a paddle

The traditional method of travel on the Amazon Basin's many rivers is to paddle a canoe. They may be carved out from logs, or made from planks of wood, such as balsa. The Xingu peoples (left) live and fish by the river.

Deforestation

The biggest threat to the Amazon Rainforest is deforestation, a process in which trees are cleared, leaving nowhere for Indigenous peoples and wildlife to live. The forest is being cut down for logging, road building, and to make way for farms. If cleared, the rich diversity of the rainforest will be lost. Today, strict laws limit deforestation in some parts, although other areas continue to be cleared.

2001

2019

Satellite surveillance
About a fifth of the Amazon Rainforest has been cut down in the last 40 years. The Brazilian government uses satellite images to monitor the rate at which the rainforest is being cleared. The satellites can see changes in the colour of the ground, which indicates where trees have been cut down. The images above track deforestation in a section of the rainforest between 2001 and 2019.

Divisive roads
Roads were first cut into the rainforest in the 1970s. The highways create barriers within the forest that make it difficult for animals to move around as much as they need. Many animals are killed by traffic. Highways also provide access roads for illegal loggers.

Around 13,208 sq km
(5,100 sq miles) of Brazil's Amazon Rainforest was lost between August 2020 and July 2021.

Logging
Another major cause of deforestation is logging. The hardwood trees of the Amazon Rainforest are used for making furniture that is sold around the world. The loggers cut down a few of the largest trees and then move on to another area.

EYEWITNESS

Txai Suruí
Climate activist Txai Suruí, from the Suruí community in Brazil, is one of many Amazonian people to experience the devastating effects of climate change. In 2021, at an international climate conference, she called on world leaders to take action, highlighting how deforestation has increased at an alarming rate in recent years.

Secondary forest

Once the primary, or original, rainforest has been cut down, a secondary forest starts to grow. This has fewer trees, and only some of the animals that once thrived in the primary forest. In time, smaller trees and plants begin to grow in the secondary forest. Many plants need animals to spread their seeds, and as many of the animals do not exist any longer, some of the plants they supported will never return naturally.

Primary forest has a thick canopy, an understorey of bushes, and a diverse animal population.

After deforestation, cut logs are burned to clear the ground.

Grasses and other plants appear.

Small trees and shrubs start to grow.

Secondary forest has a thinner canopy and fewer plants growing underneath.

Slash and burn

A helicopter carrying environmental officers is flying in to arrest thieves who have cleared trees illegally for farming. The main method of clearing the forest is called slash and burn, a process in which trees are cut up and burned. The ash makes the soil a little more fertile, but only for a few years.

Mining and damming

The Amazon region is not only home to forest but also to cities and other developments that need to be supplied with power and resources. Dams across many of the Amazon's largest rivers generate electricity, while metals and useful minerals are mined from the ground. However, these activities have an impact on both the environment and Indigenous communities in the area, which must be taken into consideration when planning new mines and dams.

Gold rush
There are gold rushes happening all over the Amazon region, with people clearing the forest to look for gold in the rocks underneath. Miners crush the rocks and wash water through them; if they are lucky, this carries away the dust and sand to reveal grains of shiny gold.

Growing fuel
Brazil is the world's leading producer of sugar cane. Raw sugar from the cane is used to make ethanol, a plant-based alternative for non-renewable fuels, such as coal. Biofuels, such as ethanol, are thought to be environmentally friendly, but creating sugar cane plantations means cutting down forests, or using land that could be used to grow food crops.

Battle for land

Many mines, dams, and oil wells occupy land in the Amazon region that belongs to Indigenous tribes. Some tribes protest over their land being destroyed for these purposes, so the government must consider the benefits of industry alongside the interests of the Indigenous communities, and what is good for the environment.

Protesters marching against the construction of the Belo Monte dam

EYEWITNESS

Ruth Buendía

In 2010, Peruvian activist Ruth Buendía worked with Indigenous communities, especially the Asháninka community, to protest against dams that had been planned for the River Ene without their consent. Eventually, the scheme was abandoned, thanks to Buendía's efforts. She was awarded the Goldman Environmental Prize in 2014 for her work.

Carrying oil

This pipe is carrying crude oil pumped from a well in the rainforests of Ecuador. This valuable resource will be used to make fuel, chemicals, plastic, and medicines. However, pipes and wells can leak, and the spilt oil pollutes the area's rivers, damaging wildlife and causing health problems for those who live in the forests.

Damming the river

The Amazon Basin's largest mega-dam – the Belo Monte on the Xingu River – is a controversial project. Completed in 2019, it promised energy security for Brazil but has yet to achieve its potential. The dam created a reservoir that flooded parts of the rainforest and forced many Indigenous peoples and wildlife to move out of the area.

Mighty mine

The Carajás Mine in Brazil is the largest iron ore mine in the world. About 3,000 people work there, digging out rock that contains iron and other metals. Once all the ore has been dug out, the mine will be filled and a new rainforest will be planted to cover the bare ground.

Endangered species

Although the Amazon rainforest has existed for more than 50 million years, it is constantly changing. Animal and plant species evolve and new ones appear. Today, the forest is home to more than 3 million species of plants and animals. Yet, as human activity continues to damage the rainforest, a number of species are running out of places in which to survive. Many of these species are in danger of becoming extinct.

The redness of the face indicates strength to other monkeys.

English monkey
Local people call the uakari monkey the English monkey because it looks like a sunburnt tourist. Living in the trees above flooded forests in Peru, it climbs to the ground in search of seeds only when the floodwater has drained away. Hunting is the reason that its population is now in decline.

White-blotched ray
White-blotched rays live on pebbly riverbeds where they hunt for snails and crabs. They live only in the Xingu River in Brazil, which meets the Amazon River near its mouth. The new electricity-generating dam built across the Xingu has made the river deeper. This may reduce feeding areas for the rays.

Giant anteater
The giant anteater rips open the nests of ants and termites and licks up the insects inside with its sticky, 60-cm- (24-in-) long tongue. The anteater is vulnerable to extinction, partly because it is too slow to run away from forest fires, which are becoming more common in the region

Termite hill

Black-and-white stripes on flank

Orinoco crocodile

The Orinoco crocodile is one of the world's most endangered reptiles. There may be only 1,000 left. They are so rare that very little is known about them. Although they look ferocious, these crocodiles mainly eat fish.

The thin and narrow snout is slightly upturned.

Bright blue plumage

Blue birds

The hyacinth macaw is the largest parrot in the Amazon Rainforest. It is about 1 m (3.3 ft) long from its hooked beak to the tip of its long tail feathers. There are now fewer than 5,000 of these birds left in the wild. Its size and plumage make it a target for bird trappers, who sell the parrots as pets.

White stripes and spots run along its back.

Pacarana

This shy, leaf-eating animal is the last surviving relative of giant, 3-m- (10-ft-) long rodents that lived in the Amazon region about eight million years ago. Family groups of three or four pacaranas climb through the trees, using their long whiskers to feel their way. Pacaranas are becoming scarce because the forests of the western Amazon in which they live are being cut down by farmers.

Modern industry

The Amazon Basin provides many Amazonians with jobs. This helps local communities to build homes, schools, and hospitals. The biggest industry in the region is agriculture and other types of food production. In the future, industries may grow around new products the forest holds.

Around six per cent of soya beans grown in South America are consumed by humans.

Fishing
The Amazon River provides fish for millions of people. The largest fish, the arapaima, is regarded as a delicacy because it has few bones in it and can be cut into thick steaks. But so many wild arapaima have been taken from the river that the Brazilian government has made it illegal to catch them.

Palm oils
The fruits of palm trees are a traditional food for some Amazonians, but they are also grown for the oil they contain. The oil is used in different products and even in fuels. However, palm oil farms have sometimes caused environmental problems in the region because of widespread deforestation.

Palm oil and fruits

Soya bean farming
This huge farm in the cerrado grasslands south of the Amazon Rainforest grows only soya beans. Farms like this dot many parts of the Amazon region. Between 70 per cent and 90 per cent of the crop is used as animal feed. Brazil is the world's largest producer of soya beans.

Cattle ranches

There are about 80 million cattle in the Amazon region and many millions more in the surrounding hills. Cattle ranches – which include land for growing soya to feed the cattle – are the major cause of deforestation in the area.

> **EYEWITNESS**
>
> **Marina Silva**
> Brazilian politician Marina Silva is one of the strongest advocates for the protection of the Amazon Rainforest. While working as Brazil's environment minister, Silva fought against illegal logging and vast cattle ranches to combat the deforestation of the rainforest.

Medicinal plants

This researcher is talking to a local shaman (healer) to find out which plants he uses to make traditional medicines. The drug curare was discovered in an Amazonian plant. Tribes in the forest would use it as a poison, but in the 1940s, surgeons began to use it to relax patients' muscles during surgery.

Conservation

The Amazon Rainforest needs protection from the harm caused by human activities. Scientists, working with Indigenous peoples, try and figure out what the forest and its inhabitants need to thrive. Conservationists work to repair and protect habitats, while lawyers and politicians set rules for people to live and work in the forest.

Replanting
When a tall tree falls down in the forest, it leaves a gap that is filled up by other plants. Eventually a new tree fills the space in the canopy. Scientists are trying to recreate this process. The plants being grown in the nursery above will be used to replenish the Atlantic Forest.

Wood storks arrive from their wintering grounds.

Applying science
The scientist here – an ecologist – is tracking a monkey in the Ecuadorian Amazon by following the radio signals emitted from a device attached to the animal. The research conducted by ecologists shows the damage caused when humans alter the natural habitat.

Climate change
The average temperature in the Amazon is slowly rising because of climate change. There is also less rainfall, which will affect the Indigenous peoples, plants, and animals. If the forest begins to dry out, there will be more forest fires and many species will not be able to survive. Scientists all over the world are trying to stop this process.

Protecting cultures

The traditional cultures of the Amazon region are also threatened by deforestation, mining, and logging, and they need to be protected. A fifth of the rainforest belongs to different tribes that have lived in the area for thousands of years. Big portions of tribal land have been taken over illegally by farmers. Indigenous activists from the Amazon region are raising their voices against the destruction of their land and the killing of their people.

Protests after two indigenous people were killed in Brazil

Conservation sites

Many storks and egrets migrate to the Pantanal wetland every year. If this area was drained to make way for fields, these birds would have nowhere to live. The best way to protect animal species is to conserve their habitats. But today, only 2 per cent of the Pantanal is protected in reserves.

EYEWITNESS

Nemonte Nenquimo
In 2019, Nemonte Nenquimo led her people – who form the Indigenous Waorani nation in the Ecuadorian Amazon – in a court case against Ecuador's government, which planned to sell their land without their consent. The Waorani won the case, preventing the sale of their rainforest land.

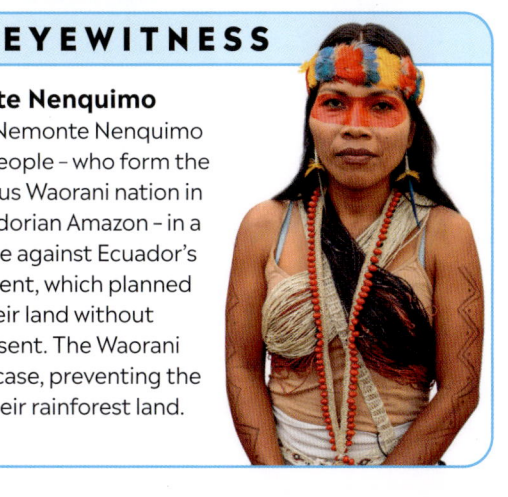

Traffic sign

With roads being built through the forest, road signs warn drivers to look out for animals, such as anteaters, that may walk onto the road. Anteaters are slow-moving creatures and may not be able to get out of the way of a fast-moving vehicle. As this species is endangered, road signs are one way to ensure they survive.

59

Ecotourism

Tourists pay to visit the Amazon Rainforest, and some of the money they spend goes to the local people and towards conservation programmes. Inviting visitors to explore the rich habitat raises awareness of this rainforest, and is more beneficial than cutting it down to build cities and farms. This region's holiday industry is a prime example of ecotourism. The best of it is sustainable, and is ethically run in partnership with Indigenous communities.

Hotel built on stilts in the river

Forest resort
Ecotourists stay in comfortable hotels, known as lodges. The buildings are designed to be highly energy efficient so they do not use a lot of fuel, which has to be brought in by boat. Waste is also kept to a minimum.

Straight sticks sharpened into arrows

Meeting the locals
Tour groups visit Indigenous communities, where the residents share their skills and way of life, such as how they use forest plants to make the things they need. The visits provide a chance for Amazonians to share their knowledge as well as create an income.

Walking among the trees
Rope walkways and viewing platforms are built high up in the canopy of tall trees. They allow visitors to see the birds, monkeys, insects, and plants that can't be seen from the forest floor.

Guided tours
Most visitors to the Amazon Rainforest come to see the wildlife. Local guides take tourists on walks through the rainforest or on boat tours. The tourists travel in canoes, not speedboats, as high-speed vessels create waves that would damage the riverbanks. Some guided tours take place at night, when caimans and other nocturnal animals are active.

EYEWITNESS

The Cofán people
The Cofán people live in Ecuador's Amazon forests. They run ecotours for visitors who want a first-hand experience of Indigenous culture. Guests stay in a Cofán village, travel in their dug-out canoes, and learn about their traditional way of life. These ecotours give the Cofán people a source of income to maintain their ancestral land.

Binoculars for viewing wildlife

Saving the animals
Tourists in the Amazon Rainforest can help park rangers to look after endangered animals before they are released into the wild. Visitors to Peru are seen here feeding milk to baby manatees. This example of ecotourism helps raise money so that more of the rare manatees can be raised and protected.

Farming

Many fruits and nuts eaten the world over come from forest plants. In the Amazon Rainforest, local people have been growing their own crops for centuries, using traditional farming methods. Today, conservation programmes are helping them to develop new sustainable methods, so that they can grow extra crops to sell. Sustainable farms make money for the Amazon communities without causing any damage to the natural habitats.

Açaí palm

The açaí palm tree grows naturally in the swampy forests near the Amazon River's mouth. Locals harvest the tree for the soft, edible palm hearts inside its young stems. The berries also taste good, and locals use them to make juices.

Growing coffee

More than 10 million tonnes of coffee beans are sold across the world every year, and some of it is grown in the Amazon Rainforest. Farmers grow coffee beans on small bushes that are planted among the main forest trees.

Five beans grow inside a tough pod.

Coffee beans in bowl

Coffee plant berries

Cocoa

Chocolate comes from cocoa beans, which grow wild in the Amazon Rainforest. Indigenous peoples were using chocolate in food hundreds of years before it became a popular treat around the world. Today, most of the world's cocoa is grown in West Africa, but it can be grown on rainforest farms.

Brazil nuts

Despite the name, these large, tasty nuts are grown all over the Amazon region, not just in Brazil. Wild Brazil nut trees grow along riverbanks. The nuts, which are the trees' seeds, drop to the ground in a round pod. Forest rodents eat some nuts and bury the rest for later. Some of the buried nuts grow into new trees.

Agroforestry

The Amazonian farmers above are raking out chillies from the eastern Brazilian town of Tomé-açu to dry in the sunshine. The farming community there was set up by Japanese settlers 100 years ago. When the local pepper crop was killed by pests, the people of Tomé-açu decided to replant the forest trees and grow crops in their shade. This type of farming is called agroforestry.

Bananas

Pineapple

Passion fruit

Jungle fruits

Although from Southeast Asia, bananas are also grown in South America. The first pineapples came from the forests near the Pantanal wetland. Passion fruit is another Amazon plant, and the region was also home to the first tomatoes, peppers, and chillies.

Making rubber

Here a farmer is cutting a notch in a rubber tree to release a liquid called latex. This is used to make natural rubber, which is harvested on sustainable farms in the Amazon region. Making things from natural rubber creates less pollution than common artificial rubber, which is made from petroleum oil.

Amazon wonders

The Amazon region is a collection of many wonders. The mountains around the Amazon Basin were home to the most advanced civilizations in the Americas prior to the arrival of the Europeans. There are also incredible natural features down in the vast lowlands, as well as historic cities in which modern life and architecture mix with the wild Amazon Rainforest.

Iquitos
This Peruvian city is one of the most remote places on Earth. In the early 1900s, it became a major centre in the rubber industry. However, even today, its 420,000 inhabitants cannot leave town by road. They either have to get a boat downriver or catch a plane. The city is 3,600 km (2,235 miles) from the ocean, but the Amazon River is still deep enough here for ocean-going ships to dock in the city's harbour.

Mount Roraima
According to local folklore, Mount Roraima in the Guiana Highlands is the stump of a huge tree that bore all the fruits in the world until it was cut down by a demon. The mountain's rocks are 2 billion years old and were formed when South America was still connected to Africa.

Anavilhanas Archipelago
This is the largest archipelago of river islands in the world. It is a collection of 400 forested islands on the Rio Negro, upstream from the Brazilian city of Manaus.

Tumucumaque National Park
This nature reserve is the world's largest national park, and is bigger than Belgium.

Rio Negro Bridge
Completed in 2010, this 3.6 km (2.2 mile) bridge, located on the Rio Negro, is the first major road bridge on the Amazon River system.

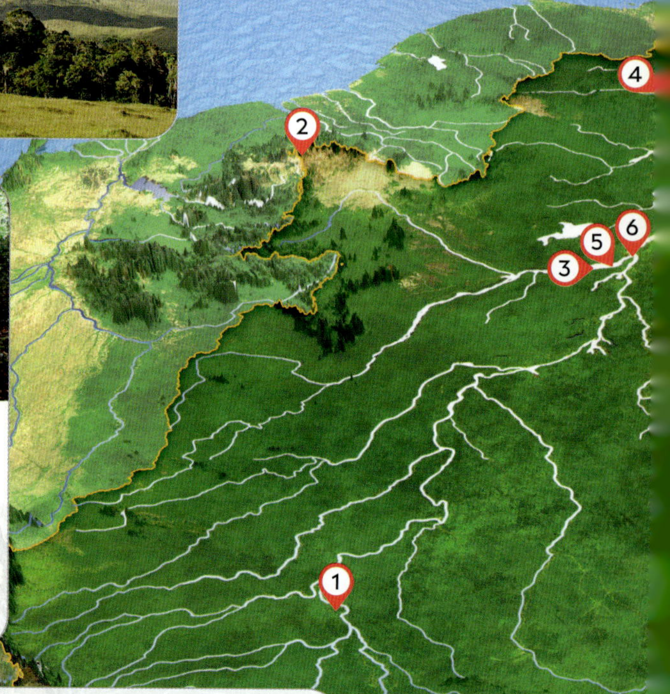

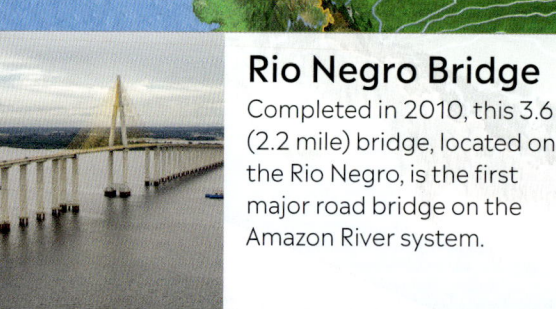

Manaus
The Teatro Amazonas opera house was built in 1884 and is still a famous landmark in the Brazilian city of Manaus. It was paid for with money from the rubber industry, the same industry that made Manaus the largest city in the Amazon Basin. Manaus is located at the meeting point of the River Amazon and the Rio Negro.

Pantanal
The Pantanal is the world's largest wetland. It forms in a hollow basin in the Brazilian Highlands that fills with rainwater flowing down from the surrounding hills. The water never gets more than about 5 m (16.4 ft) deep.

Valle de la Luna
Meaning the Valley of the Moon, the Valle de la Luna is a desert region filled with tall rock towers. The towers were created by erosion that washed away the softer clays that once filled the valley. This valley is close to La Paz, the capital city of Bolivia. They are both located on the Altiplano, a high plateau west of the Amazon Basin.

Sacred Valley
The Sacred Valley in the Peruvian Andes was the heartland of the Inca Empire. The Inca used these ancient, human-made pools – built by the people of Chanapata culture – to produce salt. The rest of the valley was used to grow maize, which was the main food in Inca cooking. The imperial Inca capital was Cusco, which is located at the valley's southern end.

Machu Picchu
The Inca city of Machu Picchu sits high up in the Andes Mountains. It was thought to be a religious centre used by the Inca king, but was largely abandoned after the collapse of the Inca Empire when the Spanish invaded in the 16th century.

Amazon facts

The Amazon region is a place of superlatives. It has the world's largest rainforest, its biggest river system, its largest river island, its widest river mouth, and its biggest tributary. Here are many more facts that show what an incredible place this region is and how record-breaking some of its animals are.

Mass of life
Biomass is a measure of how many living things exist in an area. Rainforests have the highest biomass of any land habitat. The biomass in one square mile of the Amazon Rainforest is equivalent to the weight of two Nimitz-class aircraft carriers used by the US Navy, each of which weighs nearly 97,000 tonnes.

Biodiversity
This graph shows the number of different animal species found in an average 10 sq km (4 sq miles) of the Amazon Rainforest. Just a few of the many life forms that are crowded into the forest are shown here.

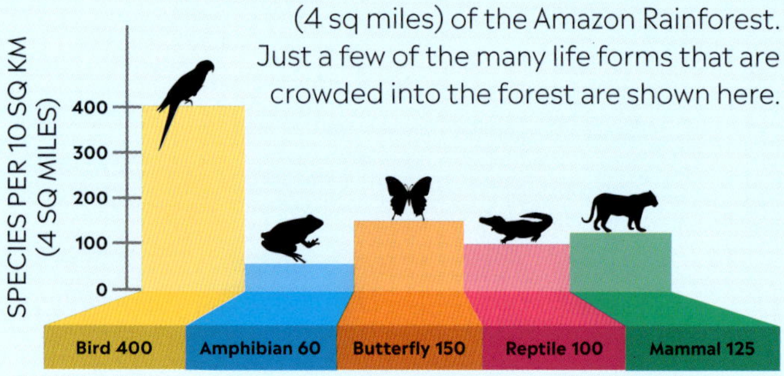

SPECIES PER 10 SQ KM (4 SQ MILES)

- Bird 400
- Amphibian 60
- Butterfly 150
- Reptile 100
- Mammal 125

Endangered species
Many Amazonian species are under threat because of damage to their habitat. The International Union for Conservation of Nature (IUCN) is monitoring species that are in danger of extinction in the region. A 2021 survey by the Science Panel for the Amazon reported that 8,000 plant species and 2,300 animal species are threatened with extinction in the Amazon.

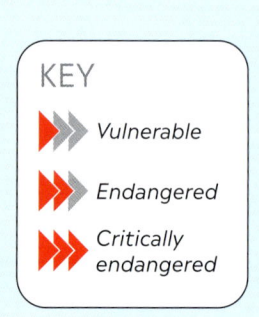

KEY
- ▶ Vulnerable
- ▶▶ Endangered
- ▶▶▶ Critically endangered

South American manatee ▶▶	Uakari monkey ▶▶	Giant anteater ▶▶
Golden lion tamarin ▶▶▶	Jocotoco antpitta ▶▶▶	Giant otter ▶▶▶
Rancho Grande harlequin frog ▶▶▶	Glaucous macaw ▶▶▶	Cherry-throated tanager ▶▶▶

LARGEST ANIMALS

The capybara is the largest rodent in the world. This species lives in the rivers and wetlands of the Amazon region. It can grow to more than 1 m (3.3 ft) in length.

Amazonian macaws are the largest types of parrot in the world. Some species can grow to about 1 m (3.3 ft) in length.

The Amazon Rainforest's 3-cm- (1.18-in-) long bullet ants are among the largest ants in the world.

The green anaconda can be found in the wetlands and the forest rivers of the Amazon region. At about 5 m (16.4 ft) long, it may not be the longest snake in the world, but it is certainly the heaviest – a fully grown anaconda can weigh up to 100 kg (220 lb).

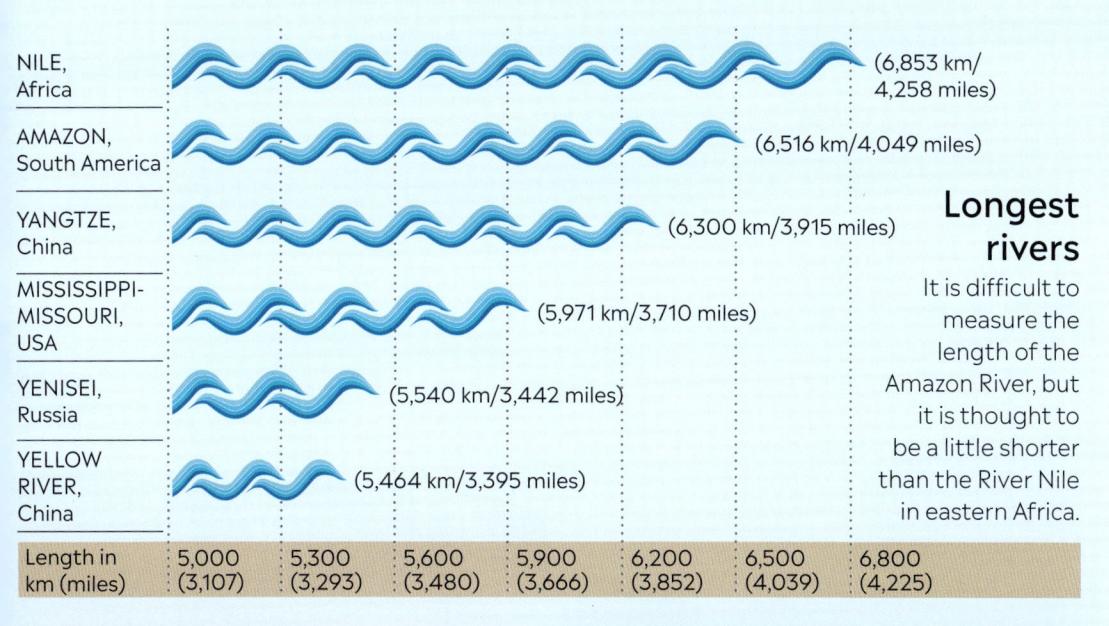

Longest rivers

River	Length
NILE, Africa	(6,853 km/4,258 miles)
AMAZON, South America	(6,516 km/4,049 miles)
YANGTZE, China	(6,300 km/3,915 miles)
MISSISSIPPI-MISSOURI, USA	(5,971 km/3,710 miles)
YENISEI, Russia	(5,540 km/3,442 miles)
YELLOW RIVER, China	(5,464 km/3,395 miles)

Length in km (miles): 5,000 (3,107); 5,300 (3,293); 5,600 (3,480); 5,900 (3,666); 6,200 (3,852); 6,500 (4,039); 6,800 (4,225)

It is difficult to measure the length of the Amazon River, but it is thought to be a little shorter than the River Nile in eastern Africa.

FAST FACTS

- The Amazon River washes a lot of soil out to sea. However, the sediment is replaced by 3.6 million tonnes of dust from the Sahara Desert, which is blown over by strong winds every year.
- When it is scared, the Amazon milk frog produces a white, milky liquid from its skin.

Amazon milk frog

- Amazonian macaws eat the clay on riverbanks to get salt and other nutrients.
- If crops are grown beneath the trees – a system called agroforestry – an area of the Amazon Rainforest can make 42 times more profit than if it was cleared for cattle pasture.
- A fungus from the Amazon region has been shown to eat plastic.
- A relative of the raccoon, the kinkajou has a prehensile tail that grips branches as it forages for insects and fruits.

Kinkajou

SMALLEST ANIMALS

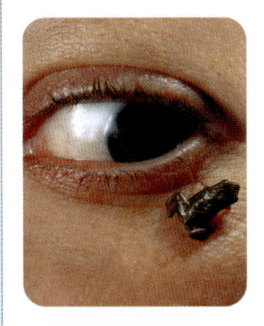

At just 1 cm (0.39 in) long, Izecksohn's toad is the smallest frog in the Amazon Rainforest.

The tiny white-bellied woodstar is 8 cm (3.14 in) long.

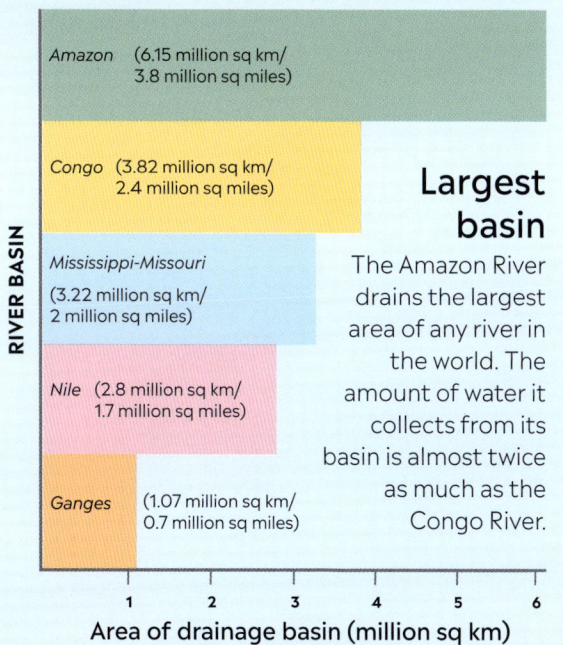

Largest basin

RIVER BASIN:
- Amazon (6.15 million sq km/3.8 million sq miles)
- Congo (3.82 million sq km/2.4 million sq miles)
- Mississippi-Missouri (3.22 million sq km/2 million sq miles)
- Nile (2.8 million sq km/1.7 million sq miles)
- Ganges (1.07 million sq km/0.7 million sq miles)

Area of drainage basin (million sq km)

The Amazon River drains the largest area of any river in the world. The amount of water it collects from its basin is almost twice as much as the Congo River.

NEW DISCOVERIES

There are parts of the Amazon that have never been properly explored by scientists. As a result, there are many animals in the rainforest that are yet to be discovered. On average, one new species is discovered in the Amazon every two days. Because these animals are new to science, almost nothing is known about them.

Monkeys are the most studied of all Amazonian wildlife, but new species are still being found. Schneider's marmoset, a primate living in the forests of Mato Grosso, Brazil, was first described in 2021.

The zombie frog, discovered in 2021, spends most of its life underground. It can only be found after it rains when males call out to attract females.

Amazon by country

The Amazon Basin covers nine separate countries. Most of the rainforest is located in Brazil, and Peru contains the next biggest section. The remaining 20 per cent is divided between the seven other countries.

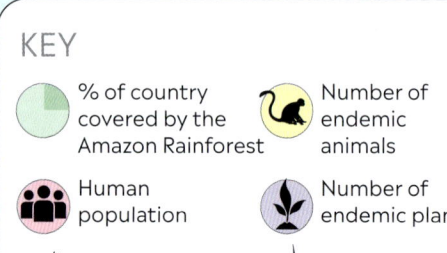

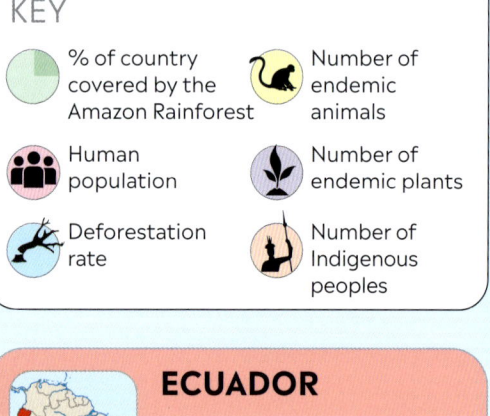

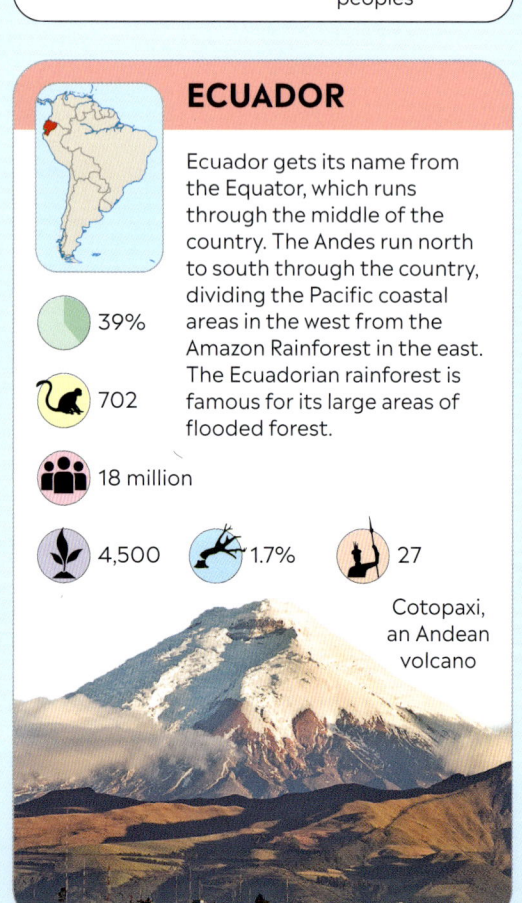

KEY
- % of country covered by the Amazon Rainforest
- Number of endemic animals
- Human population
- Number of endemic plants
- Deforestation rate
- Number of Indigenous peoples

VENEZUELA

The Llanos wetland and Guiana Highlands are located in this country. Venezuela's main forests are around the Orinoco River, which flows into the Caribbean Sea and is connected to the Amazon River near its source in Brazil.

- 52%
- 672
- 28 million
- 9,200
- 0.5%
- 26

Waterfalls at Jasper Creek

BRAZIL

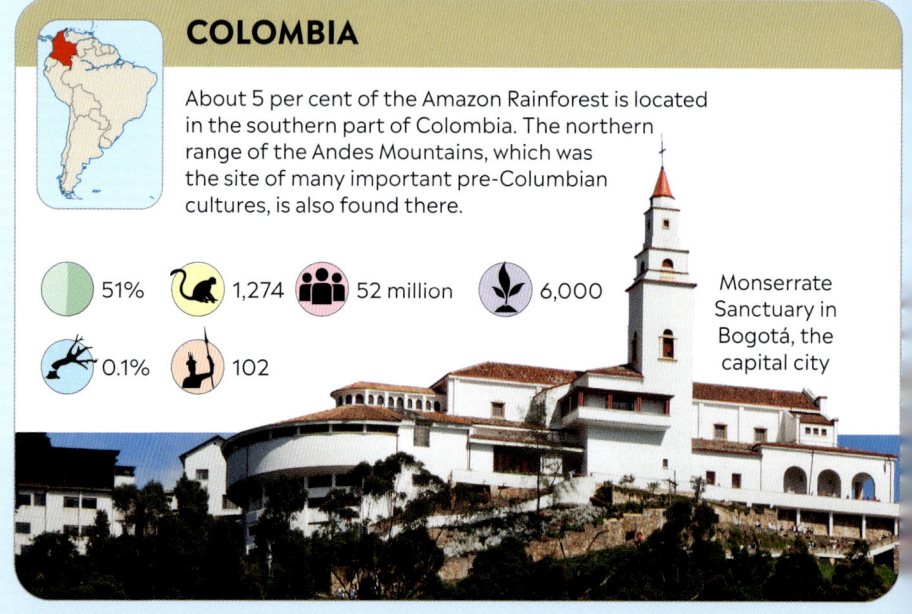

The largest country in South America, Brazil is also the fifth most populated nation in the world. Around half of Brazil is covered by the Amazon Basin. More than 60 per cent of the Amazon Rainforest is located within its borders.

Iguazu Falls, on the Iguazu River

ECUADOR

Ecuador gets its name from the Equator, which runs through the middle of the country. The Andes run north to south through the country, dividing the Pacific coastal areas in the west from the Amazon Rainforest in the east. The Ecuadorian rainforest is famous for its large areas of flooded forest.

- 39%
- 702
- 18 million
- 4,500
- 1.7%
- 27

Cotopaxi, an Andean volcano

COLOMBIA

About 5 per cent of the Amazon Rainforest is located in the southern part of Colombia. The northern range of the Andes Mountains, which was the site of many important pre-Columbian cultures, is also found there.

- 51%
- 1,274
- 52 million
- 6,000
- 0.1%
- 102

Monserrate Sanctuary in Bogotá, the capital city

SURINAME

Suriname is almost completely forested, apart from its southernmost fringe, which consists of grasslands. This country was once a Dutch colony, the only one in South America.

92% 65 600,000 2,600 0.01% 15

Central Suriname Nature Reserve

FRENCH GUIANA

French Guiana is an overseas territory of France and its people are French citizens. Much of the forested interior is uninhabited.

92% 54 312,000
1,200 0.2% 6

Maroni River

GUYANA

Once a British colony, Guyana became an independent country in 1966. Much of its land is hilly, and the southern half is covered in rainforest.

62% 122 790,000
3,500 22
0.5%

Nevado Sajama, a volcano

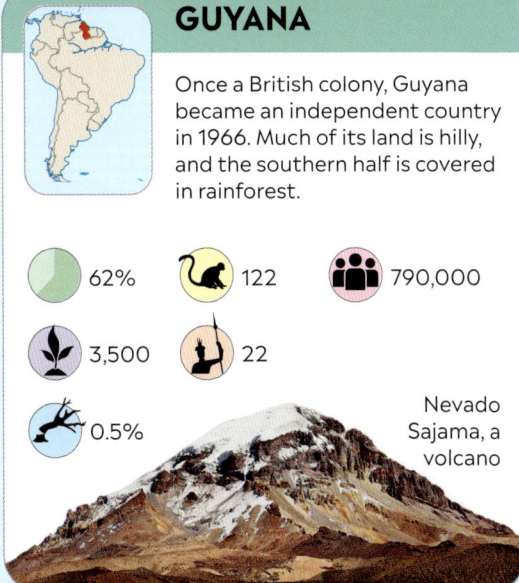

50% 4,159
215 million 25,000
6% 305

PERU

Peru contains 10 per cent of the Amazon Rainforest. It is also home to the source of the Amazon River. The eastern half of Peru is covered in lowland rainforest.

53% 1,132 34 million
8,500 0.1% 51

Urubamba Valley

BOLIVIA

Two-thirds of Bolivia lies in the Amazon Basin. Most of this area consists of high mountains, including a high plateau called Altiplano, which is covered in deserts and salt flats.

55% 243 12 million
4,000 1% 36

Kanuku Mountains

69

Glossary

Strawberry poison dart frog, an amphibian

AGROFORESTRY The practice of cultivating agricultural crops among naturally growing trees. Agroforestry helps protect natural habitats.

AMPHIBIAN A class of vertebrate that generally spends part of its life in water and has to keep its skin moist at all times. Frogs and salamanders are amphibians.

ARID Describes an area that is dry all the time.

ATLANTIC FOREST An area of rainforest in Brazil near the coast of the Atlantic Ocean.

BACTERIA Tiny organisms that are far too small to see without a microscope. Most bacteria live in natural habitats and are harmless.

BASIN A hollow area of land surrounded by hills or mountains on at least three sides.

BIODIVERSITY The variety of life – plants, animals, and fungi – that can be found in a particular place.

BIOMASS A measure of how much life is in an area. Biomass is calculated by adding up the combined weight of all life forms.

CAATINGA A type of dry forest found around the edges of the Amazon Rainforest. It has sandy soil and is filled with grasses, bushes, and small trees.

CAECILIAN An unusual amphibian that looks like a snake or worm. While most caecilians live on the forest floor, some swim in water.

CERRADO An area of mostly shrubs and grasses that grows around the edge of the Amazon Rainforest, where the rainfall is not sufficient for a full forest to grow.

CLIMATE CHANGE Long-term changes in Earth's climate and weather. This has an effect on wind, rainfall, and temperature.

CLOUD FOREST A type of tropical forest that grows on the slopes of mountains. The trees are smaller than those in a lowland jungle, and the area is often covered in fog or mist from low-lying clouds.

DECIDUOUS Plants that drop their leaves during harsh seasons. Most deciduous trees shed leaves before winter, but in the tropics they drop leaves in the hottest, driest time of the year.

DEWLAP A flap of skin that hangs down from the neck or throat.

ENDANGERED When an animal or other life form is in danger of becoming extinct.

ENDEMIC A species that occurs naturally in one place and is found nowhere else on Earth.

EPIPHYTES Plants that lack roots and grow on the branches and trunks of other, larger plants.

EVERGREEN A tree or other plant that is always covered in leaves. New leaves continue to grow even as old leaves fall off.

EXTINCT When all members of a species have died.

FLOODED FOREST A forest that is flooded with river water so the tree trunks and roots are submerged in water.

FLOODWATER Extra water from a river that overflows the river banks and covers nearby land.

GEOGRAPHY A field of science concerned with the study of the lands, features, inhabitants, and phenomena of Earth.

HABITAT A place where a plant or animal lives. Most species are adapted to live in one type of habitat, such as a rainforest.

HIGHLANDS An area of hills, mountains, and plateaux. Most highlands are mountains that have been worn down over millions of years.

HUMID Describes a climate in which the air is full of water vapour.

INDIGENOUS Someone who belongs to communities that have lived in a region for perhaps thousands of years. It can also refer to something that is produced or occurs naturally in an area.

INVERTEBRATE An animal without a backbone, such as an insect, snail, or worm. Of all the animal species known to science, at least 97 per cent are invertebrates.

LIANA FOREST A forest dominated by lianas – climbing plants that grow out of the ground and snake up around the trunks and branches of trees to reach the sunlight. Lianas use the host tree to support their own weight.

Inflated dewlap on an anole lizard

Liana wrapped around tree trunk

70

Wandering spider (predator) eats a beetle (prey)

LOGGER Someone who cuts down trees, which are turned into timber products. Some loggers are criminals because they cut down trees that are protected by law.

LOGGING An industry that provides timber for construction and paper manufacture. Most of the world's logging is conducted in forests that are grown specially to supply timber. However, the Amazon Rainforest suffers from illegal logging.

LOWLAND An area of flat land that is not very far above sea level, the point from which the heights of all land forms are measured.

MACHETE A tool with a thick cutting blade. Machetes help to cut a path through thick jungle.

MARSUPIAL A type of mammal that carries its young in a pouch on its belly. Most marsupials are from Australia and New Guinea, but a few species also live in the Americas.

NOCTURNAL Active at night.

NUTRIENT A substance that a living thing needs to survive. Plants absorb nutrients from light, air, and water, while animals get theirs by eating other life forms. Nutrients include fats and proteins.

PETROLEUM Also known as rock oil or crude oil. Petroleum is a thick black liquid pumped up from underground at oil wells. It is a mixture of chemicals created over millions of years from the remains of living things. Petroleum is then refined to make fuels, chemicals, plastics, and pharmaceuticals.

PLATEAU A flat area high above sea level.

POLLINATION The process in which pollen is delivered to a flower by an insect or other animal, or by the wind. Flowers must be pollinated to produce seeds.

POLLUTION The process by which human activities introduce harmful substances to the natural environment. Chemicals in the air, water, or soil, as well as too much light or noise, are all forms of pollution.

POPULATION In biology, a group of animals of one species that live in a particular area, such as a forest or even a single tree.

PREDATOR A hunting animal that catches and kills another animal for food.

PREHENSILE A body part that can grasp an object, and so functions like a hand or foot.

PREHISTORIC Referring to the time in a culture's history when no historical events were recorded.

PREY An animal that is hunted by a predator.

REPTILE A class of vertebrate that lays its eggs on land, and has a body covered in waterproof scales. Reptiles include snakes, lizards, turtles, and crocodiles.

RIVER SYSTEM A network of rivers that collect water from a particular region.

RODENT A small mammal that has sharp front teeth that are used for gnawing. Rodents include mice, squirrels, and guinea pigs.

Napo River, a tributary of the Amazon River

SALT FLAT A region of land that is covered in a crust of salt crystals.

SYMBIOSIS A partnership between two members of different species. Both partners help each other by providing food or protection.

TIDAL BORE A tall wave that travels up a river when the tide is very high.

TRIBUTARY A small river that flows into a larger one.

VENOMOUS Refers to venom, a poison that is injected by an animal into another one. Also used to describe animals that secrete venom.

VERTEBRATE An animal that has a backbone.

VOLCANO A mountain that develops around a crack in our planet's crust. Hot molten rock erupts out of the crack and spreads over the land as lava.

Reventador volcano, Ecuador

Index

A
activism 50, 53, 59
agriculture 17, 56-57, 62-63
agroforestry 63
air travel 49
Amazon Basin **8-9**
Amazon Cone 8
Amazon Rainforest **6-7**
  deforestation **50-51**, 56, 59
Amazon River 8, **10-11**
amphibians **32-33**
anacondas 30, 66
Anavilhanas Archipelago 64
ancient civilizations **38-39**
Andes Mountains 14, 15
animals 6-7, 66-67
  amphibians 32-33
  birds 20-21, 31, 55, 59
  endangered **54-55**, 59, 61, 66
  fish 36-37
  invertebrates 18, 24, 26-27
  mammals 22-23, 24-25, 28-29, 41
  predators 30-31
  reptiles 24, 25, 34-35
anteaters 54
ants 26, 66
arapaimas 36, 42
armadillos 24
arowanas 37

BC
basins **8-9**, 67
bats 17, 30
beaches 46
bears 24
beetles 16, 26
Belo Monte Dam, Brazil 53
biodiversity 66
biofuels 52
biomass 66
birds **20-21**, 31, 55, 59
boas 34, 42
boats 46, 49, 61
Boiling River, The 64
Bolivia 14, 15, **69**
Brazil 44, 47, 50, 68-69
  industry 52, 53, 55
  Manaus 10, 46, 48, **65**
Brazil nuts 62
bridges 48
Buendía, Ruth 53
bugs 18, 26
bush dogs 24
butterflies 27
caecilians 33
caimans 31, 34
canoes 49
capuchin monkeys 22
capybaras 29, 66
Carajás Mine, Brazil 53
carnivals 47
cassava roots 43
cats, wild 25, 31
cattle ranches 17, 57
centipedes 26
cinnamon 41
cities 6, 39, 43, 46
Ciudad Perdida 39
climate 6
climate change 58
cloud forests 12
cocoa 62
Cofán people 61
coffee 62
Colombia 16, 39, 42, **68**
conservation 58-59, 60-61
Cousteau, Jacques 15
crickets 26
crocodiles 55

DEFGH
dams **52-53**
deforestation **50-51**, 56, 59
dolphins 11, 28, 41
drought 9
dry forests 12
eagles 31
ecotourism **60-61**
Ecuador 41, **68**
electricity 46
endangered species **54-55**, 59, 61, 66
epiphytes 19
explorers 20, **40-41**, 42
falcons 21
farming 17, 56-57, 62-63
festivals 45, 47
fish **36-37**
fishing 17, 21, 56
forests **6-7**, **12-13**
French Guiana 69
frogs 18, 32-33, 67
fruits 63
fuels 52, 53
fungi 19
gods and goddesses 42-43
gold 39, 43, 52
Guiana Highlands 9, 14, 68
Guyana 69
herons 21
history 38-39, 40-41, 42-43
horses 49
hospitals 46
howler monkeys 23
hummingbirds 16, 20
hunting 45

IJLM
Inca Empire 38-39, 43, 65
Indigenous peoples **44-45**, 49
  activism 53, 59
  ancient 38-39, 40
  farming 60, 62, 63
industry 52-53, **56-57**
invertebrates 18, 24, **26-27**
Iquitos, Peru 6, 47, **64**
jaguars 31
lakes 14-15
lilies 16-17
lizards 17, 34
llamas 15, 49
Llanos 16-17
logging 50
lost cities 39, 43
macaws 20, 55, 66
Machu Picchu 38-39, 65
mammals 22-23, 24-25, 28-29, 41
manatees 28-29
Manaus, Brazil 10, 46, 48, 65
Marajoara people 38
marmosets 23
marsupials 29
Matis tribe 44
medicine 45, 57
mining **52-53**
Molina, Gonzalo Cardona 21
monkeys 13, **22-23**, 54, 67
mountains 14-15
Muisca people 39
mycorrhizal networks 19
myths 42-43

NPR
Nenquimo, Nemonte 59
nests 21, 54
nuts 62
ocelots 25
oil 53, 56
otters 29
owl monkeys 23
owls 43, 67
pacaranas 55
palm oils 56
palm trees 12, 56, 62
Pantanal 16-17, 59, 65
Peru 11, 14, 48, **69**
  Iquitos 6, 47, **64**
  see also Inca Empire
piranhas 36
plants **18-19**, 62-63
  for medicine 45, 57
  see also trees
poisonous animals 18, 32-33
Portugal 40, 41
praying mantises 27
predators 30-31
rainfall 8
rainforests **6-7**
rays 36, 54
reforestation 58
reptiles **34-35**
  snakes 25, 30, 66
Rio Negro 10
rivers **10-11**, 67
roads 48, 50, 59
rock paintings 39
rodents 29
roots 13, 19, 43
Roraima, Mount 14, 64
rubber trees 41, 63

ST
Sachamama 42
Sacred Valley, Peru 65
salamanders 33
Salar de Uyuni, Bolivia 15
Salazar, Picuruta 11
salt flats 15
Schaan, Denise 38
schools 47
sharks 37
Sieggreen, Marcy 33
Silva, Marina 57
slavery 40
snakes 25, 30, 34-35, 66
soccer 47
songbirds 21
Souza, Lesley de 37
soya beans 56
Spain 40
spider monkeys 22
spiders 27, 30
stingrays 36
stinkbirds 21
strangler figs 18
sugar cane 52
surfing 11
Suriname 69
Suruí, Txai 50
symbiosis 19
tamarins 23
tapirs 25, 28
tetras 37
Titicaca, Lake 14-15
toads 32
toucans 20
tourism 46, 60-61
Trans-Amazonian Highway 48
travel **48-49**
trees 12-13, 16, 43, 62
  deforestation 50-51, 58
  rainforest layers 6, 51
  rubber 41, 63
  walkways 61
tributaries 10, 11
Trujillo, Fernando 28
Tumucumaque National Park, Brazil 64
turtles 35

UVWXY
underwater trees 13
Uru people 14
Valle de la Luna, Bolivia 65
Venezuela 14, 16, **68**
villages 14, 47
vine snakes 35
vipers 25, 35
Waorani people 59
waterfalls 9
wetlands **16-17**
worms 24
Xingu peoples 45, 47
yapoks 29

Acknowledgments

The publisher would like to thank the following people with their help with making the book: Ashwin Khurana, Aman Kumar, and Sheryl Sadana for text editing; Simon Mumford for illustrating maps; Georgina Palffy and the DK London Diversity, Equity, and Inclusion team for authenticity checks; Saloni Singh for the jacket; Elizabeth Wise for indexing; and Carron Brown for proofreading.

The publisher would like to thank the following for their kind permission to reproduce their images:
(Key: a-above; b-below/bottom; c-centre; f-far; l-left; r-right; t-top)

1 Dreamstime.com: Ammit. **2 Corbis:** DPA / Rolf Wilms (cb); Layne Kennedy (b). **Dorling Kindersley:** The Natural History Museum, London (c). **Dreamstime.com:** Amwu (tl). **Getty Images:** Mauricio Duenas / AFP (tl); Photodisc / Alex Cao (tc). **Thomas Marent:** (cl/ Fungus beetle). **2-3 Dreamstime.com:** Rinus Baak (t). **3 Dreamstime.com:** 44kmos (tr); Eric Gevaert (c). **4 Alamy Stock Photo:** Westend61 GmbH (tl). **Dreamstime.com:** Andrea Poole (bl); Isselee (crb); Viktarm (cl); Dolphfyn (cr); **SuperStock:** Ton Koene / VWPics / Visual & Written (br). **5 SuperStock:** Iberfoto (tr). **6 Getty Images:** De Agostini (bl). **8 Dreamstime.com:** Antares614 (bc). NASA: GSFC (bl). **9 Alamy Stock Photo:** Lee Dalton (tr). **Corbis:** Stephanie Maze (br). **Photoshot**: Imagebroker.net (cr). **10-11 Corbis:** Layne Kennedy. **10 Alamy Stock Photo:** age fotostock / Alvaro Leiva (tl). **11 Alamy Stock Photo:** Reuters / Stringer Brazil (cra); Visual&Written SL (c). **ESA:** Contains modified Copernicus Sentinel data (2017), processed by ESA, CC BY-SA 3.0 IGO (cl). **12 Alamy Stock Photo:** BrazilPhotos.com (cl). **Getty Images:** Photographer's Choice (t). **12-13 Alamy Stock Photo:** BrazilPhotos.com. **13 Alamy Stock Photo:** Robert Fried (cra). **Corbis:** Minden Pictures / Kevin Schafer br). **Dreamstime.com:** Kschua (cb). **Getty Images / iStock:** Klebercordeiro (tc). **14-15 Alamy Stock Photo:** Zoonar GmbH (t). **14 Alamy Stock Photo:** Martin Harvey (br). **Corbis:** Galen Rowell (cl). **15 Alamy Stock Photo:** David Noton Photography (cl). **Corbis:** Alison Wright (br). **Getty Images:** Bachrach / Archive Photos (cr). **16 Alamy Stock Photo:** blickwinkel (bc).**16-17 SuperStock:** Minden Pictures (c). **17 Corbis:** DPA / Rolf Wilms (cla); Theo Allofs (tr). **Getty Images:** Carol Farneti Foster / Photodisc (tc). **Glowimages:** jspix (bl). **18 Alamy Stock Photo:** Morley Read (cr). **Corbis:** Minden Pictures / Mark Moffett (tl). **Thomas Marent:** (bl). **19 Alamy Stock Photo:** Jacques Jangoux (br). **Corbis:** Minden Pictures / Mark Moffett (tr). **20 Alamy Stock Photo:** Westend61 GmbH (tl). **Dreamstime.com:** David Davis (c); Steffen Foerster (bl); Lukas Blazek (bc); Hotshotsworldwide (clb). **20-21 Dreamstime.com:** Rinus Baak (c). **21 Alamy Stock Photo:** Images & Stories (c); Kuttig - Travel (br). **Chris Jiménez:** (tl). **Dreamstime.com:** 44kmos (cr); Hotshotsworldwide (tc). **Photoshot:** NHPA (tr). **Women for Conservation:** Isabella Cortes Lara (bl). **22 Alamy Stock Photo:** Morley Read (tl/Leaves). **Corbis:** Minden Pictures / Thomas Marent (cla); Minden Pictures / Pete Oxford (clb). **22-23 Dreamstime.com:** Eric Gevaert (b). **23 Corbis:** AsiaPix / Disc Pictures (cla); Minden Pictures / Murray Cooper (r). **Dreamstime.com:** Parin Parmar (cr/Background Leaves). **Photoshot:** Picture Alliance (tc). **24 Alamy Stock Photo:** Amar and Isabelle Guillen - Guillen Photo LLC (bl); Juniors Bildarchiv GmbH (br). **Corbis:** Kevin Schafer (cra). **FLPA:** Photo Researchers (tl). **25 Alamy Stock Photo:** William Mullins (tc). **Dreamstime.com:** Andrea Poole (br). **26 Alamy Stock Photo:** Magica (clb/Euchroma gigantea); The Natural History Museum (clb/Titan Beetle). **Corbis:** Minden Pictures / Christian Ziegler (tl). **FLPA:** Photo Researchers (crb). **Thomas Marent:** (clb). **26-27 Getty Images**: (b). **27 Corbis:** Minden Pictures / Piotr Naskrecki (tr). **Dorling Kindersley:** The Natural History Museum, London (tl, ca). **Dreamstime.com:** Amwu (br). **Getty Images / iStock:** ViniSouza128 (cr). **Thomas Marent:** (crb). **28 Corbis:** Minden Pictures / Kevin Schafer (clb). **Credit ©:** Kike Calvo (bl). **28-29 naturepl.com:** Doug Perrine. **29 Alamy Stock Photo:** Prisma Bildagentur AG (tr). **Phil Myers, Animal Diversity Web (http://animaldiversity.org):** (br). **Science Photo Library:** John Devries (crb). **30 Photoshot:** NHPA (bl). **Science Photo Library:** Dr Morley Read (tl). **Jerry Young:** (cb). **30-31 Dreamstime.com:** Ammit (c). **31 naturepl.com:** Nick Garbutt (tr). **Rex Features:** Gerard Lacz (br). **32 Alamy Stock Photo:** Nature Picture Library / Pete Oxford (clb). **Dreamstime.com:** Amwu (bl); Danolsen (c); Dirk Ercken (tl, bc); Isselee (br). **33 123RF.com:** Morley Read (clb). **Dreamstime.com:** Isselee (b). **33 Angi Nelson:** (t). **Detroit Zoological Society:** (tl). **Dreamstime.com:** Isselee (bc, br); Mgkuijpers (bl). **FLPA:** Photo Researchers (crb). **34 Alamy Stock Photo:** Morley Read (tl). **Corbis:** Minden Pictures / Pete Oxford (br). **Dreamstime.com:** Isselee (c); Mgkuijpers (clb). **35 Getty Images:** Edelcio Muscat (tc). **Igor Siwanowicz:** (b). **36 Alamy Stock Photo:** Juniors Bildarchiv GmbH (tl); WaterFrame (cr). **Pittsburgh Zoo & PPG Aquarium:** (b). **37 Alamy Stock Photo:** Joshua Hee (clb). **Getty Images:** Alexander Safonov (c); Photo by K S Kong (c). **Lesley S. de Souza:** Courtesy of Lesley de Souza (cra). **38 Alamy Stock Photo:** Heritage Image Partnership Ltd (tl). **Denise Schaan:** André dos Santos (cr). **38-39 Glowimages:** Hermes Images (b). **39 Dreamstime.com:** Ildipapp (crb). **Getty Images:** AFP / Mauricio Duenas (tr); Anadolu Agency (tl); National Geographic / Gordon Wiltsie (clb). **40 123RF.com:** rook76, With permission from Sociedad Estatal Correos y Telégrafos, S.A. (tr). **Science Photo Library:** Sheila Terry (clb). **41 Alamy Stock Photo:** Rolf Richardson (cl). **Getty Images:** Almir Bindilatti (tr); Antonello (tl) **Photodisc / Alex Cao** (cr). **naturepl.com:** Mark Carwardine (br). **42-43 SuperStock:** Iberfoto (tc). **42 123RF.com:** ammit (br). **Artwork (c) Christine Marsh, www.christinemarsh.com:** (bl). **43 Alamy Stock Photo**: RooM the Agency / Keithsutherland (cb). **Corbis:** Alison Wright (b). **Mauricio Mercadante https://www.flickr.com/photos/mercadanteweb:** (ca). **Source: Empresa Brasileira de Correios e Telégrafos:** (tr). **44 Ardea:** Nick Gordon (cl). **44-45 © Survival International:** (b). **45 Alamy Stock Photo**: Pulsar Imagens (bc). **Corbis:** Ueslei Marcelino / Reuters (c, tr). **SuperStock:** Jan Sochor / age fotostock (tl). **46 Alamy Stock Photo:** peruvianpictures.com (bl); Rolf Richardson (tl). **Photoshot:** NHPA (cla). **46-47 Alamy Stock Photo:** James Davis Photography (bc). **47 Alamy Stock Photo:** Paul Harris / John Warburton-Lee Photography (t); Rolf Schulten / imageBROKER (br). **www.brasil.gov.br:** Chico Batata / Agecom - AM (cr). **48 Alamy Stock Photo:** Paul Springett 05 (bl). **Dreamstime.com:** Alex Braga (cla). **Getty Images / iStock:** Brasil2 (tr). **48-49 SuperStock:** Ton Koene / VWPics / Visual & Written (br). **49 Alamy Stock Photo:** Larry Larsen (cra); Carlos Mora (tl). **50 Alamy Stock Photo:** PhotoStock-Israel / Shay Levy (clb); Claudia Weinmann (tl). **Getty Images:** Donald Nausbaum (cr); Paul Ellis / AFP (br). **51 Corbis:** Reuters (b). **52 Alamy Stock Photo:** Nigel Dickinson (tl). **Dreamstime.com:** Jfanchin (clb). **52-53 Shutterstock.com:** Andre Penner / AP (bc). **53 Alamy Stock Photo:** Edward Parker (cra); Stock Connection Blue (br). **Getty Images:** AFP / Antonio Scorza (tr); GTW (tl/Leaves); Martin Bernetti / AFP (cl). **54 Alamy Stock Photo**: Amazon-Images (l); VWPics / Kelvin Aitken (cr); Westend61 GmbH (b). **Shutterstock.com:** GTW (tl/ Leaves). **55 Corbis:** Minden Pictures / Roland Seitre (clb). **Dreamstime.com:** Musat Christian (r). **naturepl.com:** Pete Oxford (cla). **56 Corbis:** Reuters / Brazil / Stringer (tc). **Dreamstime.com:** Dolphfyn (cr). **56-57 Corbis**: Paulo Fridman (b). **57 Alamy Stock Photo:** Zuma Press (c). **Getty Images:** AFP / Evaristo Sa (tl). **Science Photo Library:** Alison Wright (tr). **58 Getty Images:** Brasil2 (br); Mint Images / Frans Lanting (tl). **naturepl.com:** Pete Oxford (bc). **58-59 Corbis:** Minden Pictures / Theo Allofs (c). **59 Alamy Stock Photo:** Jose Giribas / Süddeutsche Zeitung Photo (bl). **Corbis:** Frans Lanting (br). **Science Photo Library:** Max Alexander (tl). **60 Alamy Stock Photo:** Jan Carroll (c). **Getty Images:** WIN-Initiative (bl). **60-61 Getty Images:** Nigel Pavitt (c). **61 Alamy Stock Photo:** Paul Springett C (tr). **Getty Images:** National Geographic / Richard Olsenius (br). **Getty Images / iStock:** Alejomiranda (cr). **62 Alamy Stock Photo:** Ammit (bl); MNS Photo (crb); Fernanda Preto (br). **Photoshot:** Nigel Smith (tl). **63 Corbis:** Minden Pictures / Luciano Candisani (b). **Dreamstime.com:** Goodween123 (cl); Viktarm (cra). **Getty Images:** Kam & Co. (tr); UniversalImagesGroup (tl). **64 123RF.com:** Alexandre Braga (bc). **Alamy Stock Photo:** Aaron Chervenak (cb). **Dreamstime.com:** Anatolii Aleksieiev (c); Debra Law (tr). **Getty Images:** Alex Robinson (clb). **64-65 Corbis:** Minden Pictures / Kevin Schafer. **65 Dreamstime.com:** Brizardh (ca); Gunter Hoffmann (tr). **66 Dreamstime.com:** Amaiquez (cra); Pablo Hidalgo (crb). **66-67 Corbis:** Minden Pictures / Kevin Schafer. **67 Antoine Fouquet:** (br). **Corbis**: Minden Pictures / Mark Moffett (cl). **Dr. Rodrigo Costa Araújo:** @amazonmarmosets (bl). **Dreamstime.com:** Alslutsky (cra); Feeding White-bellied Woodstar (clb). **68-69 Corbis:** Minden Pictures / Kevin Schafer. **Dreamstime.com:** Attila Jandi (c). **68 Dreamstime.com:** Alexandre Fagundes De Fagundes (br); Natursports (bl). **Thomas Marent:** (tr). **69 123RF.com:** Paweł Opaska (c). **Corbis:** Remi Benali (tr). **Dreamstime.com:** Kseniya Ragozina (bl). **Getty Images:** Ariadne Van Zandbergen (tl); Danita Delimont (br). **70-71 Corbis:** Minden Pictures / Kevin Schafer. **70 123RF.com:** Dirk Ercken (tl). **Thomas Marent:** (br). **71 123RF.com:** ammit (br); Morley Read (tl). **Dreamstime.com:** Kseniya Ragozina (tr).

Wallchart: **Alamy Stock Photo:** Amazon-Images fcrb, James Davis Photography bc, Pulsar Imagens (bl); **Corbis:** Layne Kennedy cla; **Dreamstime.com:** 44kmos fcl, Dolphfyn crb/ (Oil Palm Fruit), Hotshotsworldwide c, cl, Isselee cr, Viktarm crb/ (Passion fruit); **Getty Images:** Gordon Wiltsie fcra, Kam & Co. fcrb/ (Bananas); **naturepl.com:** Doug Perrine clb; **Science Photo Library:** Max Alexander (bc/Protest); Sheila Terry tr; **Shutterstock.com:** GTW (br); **Source: Empresa Brasileira de Correios e Telégrafos:** cra; **Jerry Young:** cr/ (Vampire Bat).

All other images © Dorling Kindersley
For further information see: www.dkimages.com

WHAT WILL YOU EYEWITNESS NEXT?

Packed with pictures and full of facts, DK Eyewitness books are perfect for school projects and home learning.

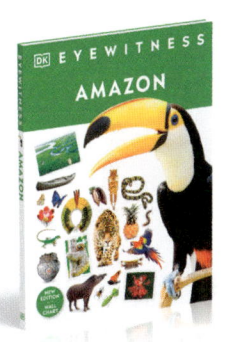

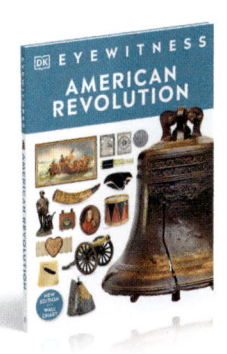

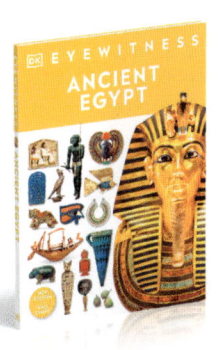

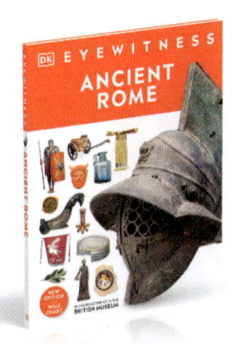

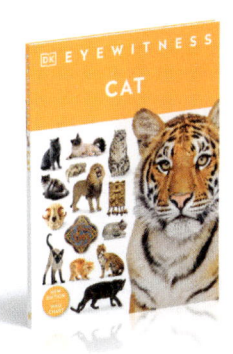

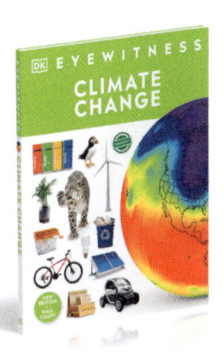

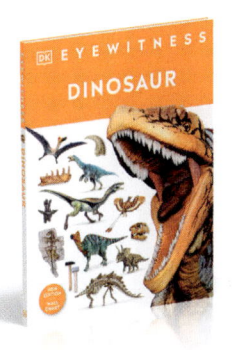

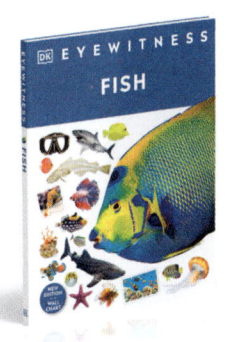

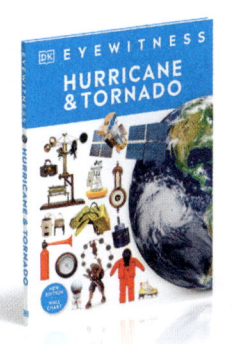

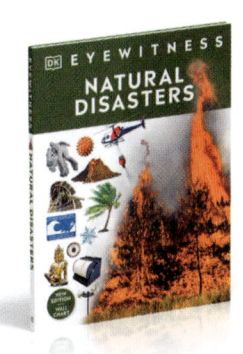

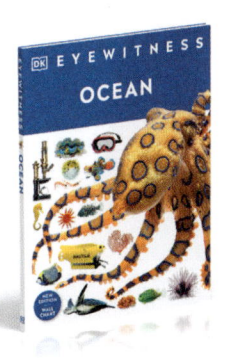

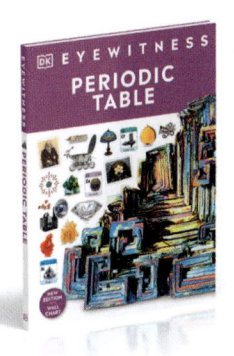

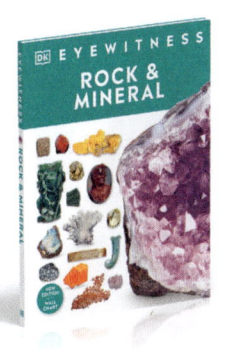

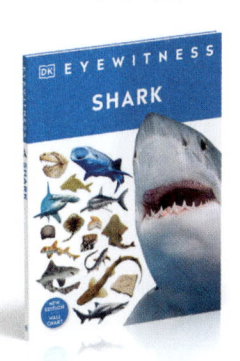

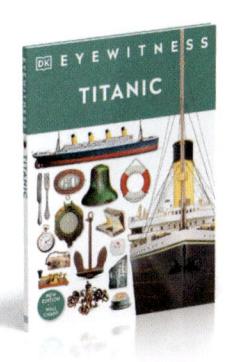

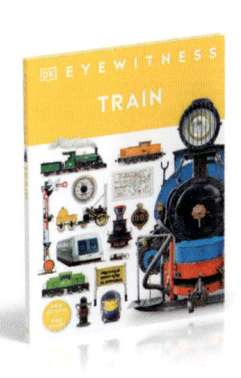

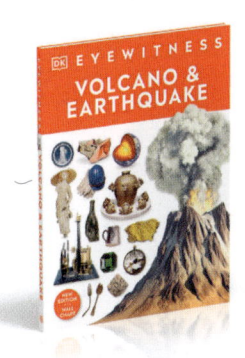

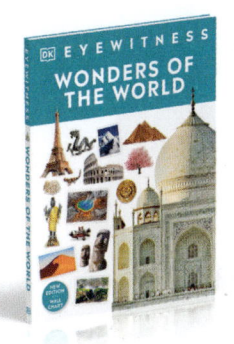

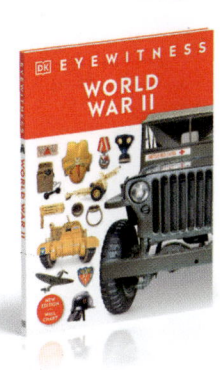

Also available:

- Eyewitness Ancient Greece
- Eyewitness Animal
- Eyewitness Bible Lands
- Eyewitness American Civil War
- Eyewitness Crystals & Gems

- Eyewitness Early People
- Eyewitness Forensic Science
- Eyewitness Football
- Eyewitness Fossil
- Eyewitness Horse

- Eyewitness Human Body
- Eyewitness Insect
- Eyewitness Islam
- Eyewitness Knight
- Eyewitness Planets
- Eyewitness Reptile

- Eyewitness Shakespeare
- Eyewitness Tudor
- Eyewitness Universe
- Eyewitness Victorians
- Eyewitness Viking
- Eyewitness World War I

DK For the curious